Many Shades of Wisdom

VOLUME I

Many Shades of Wisdom

VOLUME I

Asif Shakoor

RESOURCE *Publications* • Eugene, Oregon

MANY SHADES OF WISDOM
Volume I

Copyright © 2026 Asif Shakoor. All rights reserved. Except for brief quotations in critical publications or reviews, no part of this book may be reproduced in any manner without prior written permission from the publisher. Write: Permissions, Wipf and Stock Publishers, 199 W. 8th Ave., Suite 3, Eugene, OR 97401.

Resource Publications
An Imprint of Wipf and Stock Publishers
199 W. 8th Ave., Suite 3
Eugene, OR 97401

www.wipfandstock.com

PAPERBACK ISBN: 979-8-3852-7285-3
HARDCOVER ISBN: 979-8-3852-7286-0
EBOOK ISBN: 979-8-3852-7287-7

Contents

Introduction

A lifetime of proverbial reflection written over time inspired me to write this book. "Many Shades of Wisdom" is a work infused with Sufi mysticism, a vision of self-reflection that seeks purpose and meaning in life's journey. The book is divided into seven chapters, each seeking to reveal the subtle shades of light that form the mosaic of our existence. The spiritual nature of this work seeks a common link among philosophy, poetry, literature, and spiritual beliefs.

A Sufi poet attempts to erase the boundaries between the inner and outer worlds by lifting the veil of consciousness that hinders our mind's awareness. Walking out into the world, we shape our destiny, determining who and what we want to become. What we seek is self-realization, and what we strive for is a deeper understanding of ourselves. Who we are and what our purpose for living becomes our mind's search for wisdom. This work is my inner voice, speaking to your heart. "Many Shades of Wisdom" written on these pages are the beauty that is the soul of our humanity. The human spirit is the voice we hold sacred, and we become mindful of our search for unity in the miracle of our conscious existence.

"*The Many Shades of Wisdom*" will explore why we struggle to find happiness. It searches for truth in humanity, which binds us to wisdom and gives us the humility to overcome our human nature. The life we love is often taken for granted, but it becomes sacred when we fear losing it unexpectedly in the world. The beginning and end of time are the paths our lives must take to fulfill our spiritual journey. Is our mind awakened by our consciousness or lost in the illusions of reality to wander blind? Will the light ever reach the abyss of darkness that lurks in our human nature to touch our souls? Why do we chase fame, fortune, and wealth that only trap us further in the web of life? Why do we fear poverty and chase dreams that take us farther from ourselves? "Many Shades of Wisdom" is my search for the Self, not in the world but within myself. The vision of our existence is to look beyond and ponder the wisdom of the many shades reflected in our spirits.

A special thanks to my teacher, mentor, and friend, Prof Dan Flickstein, for taking the time to review my work and provide insightful and encouraging feedback. I have been privileged to have a teacher who inspires the best in their students. I would also like to acknowledge Andrew Menichino for sending me daily scriptures that sparked the idea for writing *Many Shades of Wisdom.* It is their gracious giving that moved my pen to write the

imprints of life's wisdom with probing
words from my whispering mind.

Wisdom is like the waves of the ocean, created when the
depth of your spirit suddenly shifts upward.

SHAKOOR

Chapter 1: Happiness, Joy, Sorrow, and Suffering

We can only spiritually appreciate the joy and happiness that come with time through suffering and sorrow. The hardships of life are the burdens we must carry and then unload when we find peace within ourselves. The light that washes away our suffering will also bring rays of hope and sunshine into our souls. Happiness only comes to those who are content with their lives by letting go of what they don't need.

Great sorrow comes to those who chase worldly pleasures that can never fulfill the greed of our human nature. We inflict the wounds of suffering upon ourselves when we are not happy with what we have and continue to desire what we can't have. The joy of living is letting go of the allure of human pleasures by untying the knots that bind you to your world.

Happiness comes to those who savor every moment and are thankful to live another day. Happiness will never find a home when the doors of compassion remain locked in your world. To suffer is our moment of wisdom to become human, but to wait for joy to come is our way of escaping our suffering. True suffering is with oneself when we continue to deceive our consciousness, even when the voice of wisdom calls for us to change our ways. "Many Shades of Wisdom" are reflected in our happiness when we bask in the joy of simplicity with conscious humility.

To suffer is our moment to reflect on life, to escape it is to wait for it to pass.

SHAKOOR

Suffering

By overcoming your sorrow, you
will reap the benefits of happiness
that will come tomorrow.

The tears in your laughter will wash
away the burden of life you hold
inside your uplifting heart.

The light of hope will reflect in your
eyes, erasing the darkness from your
soul that time brings your way.

It is the aftertaste of worldly
pleasures that, when let go, will
bring back the sweetness of our
simple existence.

The good that comes out of the evil
brings us conscious awareness of the
fragility of our human morality.

The great suffering of our spirit
comes when we sell our souls to the
wealth of worldly pleasures.

The sorrow of our hearts is the
longing for the one we love; the pain
of separation pierces us like an
unleashed arrow from the bow of the
beloved.

Those who are truly wise will remain unmoved by
feelings of happiness and suffering, fame
and disgrace, praise, and blame, gain
and loss. They will remain calm
like the eye of a hurricane.

GAUTAMA BUDDHA

Life's Burden

Lean on me when you want to shed
the tears of sorrow to wash away the
stains of your human existence.

Lean on me when your spirit is
heavy, and the world's weight is
upon your shoulders.

Lean on me when you feel the
burden of life overwhelms your heart
with a surge of emotions that drown
your soul.

Lean on me when your mind is
troubled, and your thoughts are
fragmented into a thousand pieces.

Lean on me when you lose faith in
humanity, leaving you questioning
your life's direction in this world.

Lean on me when you fall deep into
the darkness of doubt and see no
vision in the light of your spirit.

Lean on me when you are afraid to
face yourself in your mirror of Self-
reflection.

You may forget with whom you laughed,
but you will never forget
with whom you wept.

KHALIL GIBRAN

Joy of Wisdom

All we ask of you is to give us the
joy of life you bring into our souls
with your music of laughter.

All we ask of you is for you to give
us the wisdom to open our eyes and
see the beauty of your world.

All we ask of you is to guide us in
time to journey out into the world
with the rhythm in our steps.

All we ask of you is to take away the
burden of sorrow from this world
and give us the rays of sunshine to
warm our spirits.

All we ask of you is that you take
our hands and guide us on our long
path toward our worldly journey.

All we ask of you is to be true to
yourself and never hide your
reflection behind the mirrors of
illusions.

All we ask of you is just one more
day to bask in the beauty of your
creation and savor the mystical
moment in your shining light.

For a day, just for one day, talk about that
which disturbs no one and brings some
peace into your beautiful eyes.

HAFEZ, THE GIFT

Exist In Us

Will you reside in your human
compassion when others suffer, and
you suffer with them with empathy
and love?

Will you reside in the joy of living
when death is something that we
can't escape, and acceptance is the
only way out?

Will you live in your vision of
beauty and let your youthful laughter
light up your face?

Will you reside under the depths of
your emotions and let the sensual
breeze touch your soul with the love
of life?

Will you reside in your nightly
dreams and be awakened by birds
singing at the dawn of light?

Will you reside in your curiosity that
sparks your imagination and sets
your mind on fire?

Will you reside in your heart, that
will give you the walls of comfort
and love for your spirit?

The way to happiness is: keep your heart free from hate, your mind from worry. Live simply, give much. Fill your life with love. Do as you would be done by.

GAUTAMA BUDDHA

Self-revelation

Silent emotions that have not yet
been expressed feel mystical to the
heart that beats with sincerity of
love.

What is happiness to our spirit but a
pure wealth of joy that life can't
measure with time?

I am a measure of all things. If you
come to me, you shall know thy Self.
What I am, you shall be, and what
you are, I shall be. We are two ends
of a single string.

Silent thoughts, which have not yet
been spoken, carry the most
significant weight when revealed to
the mind with conscious awareness.

Life's sweet pleasures become bitter
when humanity pursues them to the
end of their existence, finding no
fulfillment.

True wisdom reflects our laughter in
a world that seems opaque to our
inner voice, which is often silenced.

The path the heart will take is to run
toward life in moments of passion
and be consumed by the desire for
love.

A meaningful existence will take us
far in life and give us time to reflect
on ourselves in quiet moments.

The world is a looking glass. It gives back to every man a true reflection of his own thoughts. Rule your mind, or it will rule you.

GAUTAMA BUDDHA

Trust Yourself

When the burden of reality breaks
our will, the strength of our character
will help us rebuild.

Follow the path of goodwill, and the
strength of our character will pull us
out of the veiled darkness of evil.

When the wisdom of truth is sinking
under our feet, then the strength of
our character will try to keep us firm
on moral ground.

When we become trapped in the
complexity of life, the strength of
our character will free us from the
world that holds us prisoner.

When the curiosity of our mind
thirsts for meaning, then the strength
of our character will give us the
knowledge to fulfill our purpose.

When our pride takes over our
humble life, then the strength of our
character will chase it away with
moral grace.

When we forget to forgive ourselves
for being human, we no longer
remember how to become humane.

Forgive and forget, but never forget to forgive.
You may find that a happier heart is the
key to a happier life.

MAHATMA GANDHI

Sound of Laughter

In the sincerity of love, we are
transformed into a spirit that seeks
love for all eternity.

In the sincerity of being human, we
live through time to seek the true
purpose of our fleeting existence.

In the sincerity of our mind, we roam
through the vastness of our
imagination to find the eternal truth
of our meaningful existence.

In the sincerity of our joy, we recite
the music of laughter that echoes
through the sound of our resounding
voice.

In the sincerity of our humanity, we
are bound to a life of virtue through
our deeds, marked by moral acts of
humility.

In the sincerity of our deeds, we are
swept away by the duty of giving to
others what we love most.

In the sincerity of our compassion,
we feel the world's emotions fall into
our hearts as we pick them up and
make them our own.

Life is a song - sing it. Life is a game - play it. Life is a challenge - meet it. Life is a dream - realize it. Life is a sacrifice - offer it. Life is love - enjoy it.

SAI BABA

Serenity

In peace, we unburden ourselves
from the heaviness of life and lift our
spirits to the joy of being loved.

In peace, we open our minds to find
the sanctuary in our inner thoughts
that keep us moving toward the path
of our conscious journey.

It is in peace that our searching eyes
long to see the beauty of this world,
which moves us closer to the path of
spiritual awakening.

In peace, we extend our hands to
embrace humanity and love the
world in the totality of grace and
wonder.

In peace, we shed our human form
and walk away from ourselves to
search for our other half to make us
whole.

In peace, we lift ourselves from the
gravity of time to raise our spirits
toward the joy of living in complete
freedom.

In peace, we achieve serenity by
seeking the path that will bring
direction into our conscious journey
through time.

> The sole art that suits me is that which, rising from unrest tends toward serenity.
>
> **ANDRE GIDE**

Less Is More

Be thankful for all that life gives
you, for it can quickly be taken away
in the blink of an eye.

Be thankful for the moment to
breathe in the splendor of life, for it
can quickly suffocate us if we don't
breathe it in with our meditative
mind.

Be thankful for what you have been
given; if you ask for more, you will
remain forever in need, and that can
never be fulfilled.

Be thankful for the ones you love;
they will bring harmony and comfort
when you need it most.

Be thankful for your health; there is
no joy in wealth when living is
riddled with pain and suffering.

Be thankful for the time you have
been given, for the journey through
life will one day come to an end.

Be thankful for what you have lost; it
will allow you to gain something
more.

For everything you have missed, you have gained something else, and for everything you gain, you lose something else.

RALPH WALDO EMERSON

I Am Within

I will be there for you when you
extend your hand to me to lift your
spirit from the depths of sorrow.

I will be there for you when there is
darkness in your eyes and when you
need the light to free your mind from
the world's blindness.

I will be there when love walks away
from yourself, and you need someone to
comfort your soul from the grief of
separation.

I will be there for you when
compassion has left humanity, and
you need someone to wash away the
sorrow that clings to your spirit.

I will be there for you when tears
flow through your eyes and rain
upon your soul with bleeding
emotions.

I will be there for you when you are
there for me; we are like two spirits
that revolve around each other's
souls.

I will be there for you to fill your cup
when emptiness leaves you no hope
for fulfillment in your thirst for life.

Whoever can't see the whole in every part plays at blind man's bluff. A wise man tastes the entire Tigris in every sip.

MIRZA GHALIB

Embraced

In the deep well of sorrow, I hold
your light in my soul to give you the
vision to walk through your
darkness.

In the deep well of life, I hold your
love in my heart so that I may feel
my emotions with your loving soul.

In the deep well of wisdom, I hold
you in my moving words, embracing
you with my mystical thoughts.

In the deep well of your universe, I
journey through your doors to escape
into the world with wings of
freedom.

In the deep well of time, I began to
grow into your beauty to live in the
comfort of the world molded by your
loving hands.

In the deep well of self-reflection, I
see myself as you see me, with eyes
of sincerity in our vision of love.

In the deep well of the spirit, I see
my soul reflected in the light of love
that burns with a mystical glow.

Be aware of your own worth, use all of your
power to achieve it. Create an ocean from
a dewdrop. Do not beg for light
from the moon; obtain it
from the spark within you.

ALLAMA MUHAMMAD IQBAL

To Shore

The sweetness of love is the water of
our existence; the passionate waves
of calling bring them to shore.

The sweetness of life is the flower of
our dreams; the passionate fragrance
stirs our emotions to bring them to
the shores of our awareness.

The sweetness of joy brings laughter
into our world; the passionate spirit
waits for happiness to get them back
to shore.

The sweetness of our journey is the
life we come to live; the passionate
sense of adventure brings us to
shore.

The sweetness of our vision becomes
the colors of Nature; the passionate
beauty of creation brings them back
to shore.

The sweetness of success is
contentment in life, the craving thirst
that brings them back to shore.

Let no man in the world live in delusion.
Without a Guru, none can cross
over to the other shore.

GURU NANAK

Let It Go

We are never redeemed until we let
go of our emotions and forgive those
who have made us suffer the most.

We are never redeemed until we shed
pride and humble ourselves by
walking softly on solid ground.

We are never redeemed until we give
up the pleasures of this world and
strive for wealth in the simplicity of
our existence.

We are never redeemed until we
open our doors to love's calling and
embrace the one who enters our
souls.

We are never redeemed until we
become guests of this world and shed
the sweet fragrance of our wisdom
into the wind.

We are never redeemed if we take
more than what we are given and
leave nothing for our spirit to grow
in the world.

The first and greatest victory is to conquer yourself; to be conquered by yourself is of all things most shameful and vile.

PLATO

Will To Peace

We can walk out into the world with
peace and purpose, guided by life's
journey with rhythm in our steps.

We can erase the boundaries between
our two worlds with a conscious will
to make peace with
our inner Self.

With peace, we can seek the true
purpose of life with the oneness of
mind, body, and spirit.

With peace, we can taste the
pureness of love, the only source of
pleasure that will heal the wounded
heart.

With peace, we can absorb the
hardships of our existence and
remain calm in the chaos of our
human emotions.

With peace, we dream of the night
that will sweep away conscious time
from the reality of our mystical
mind.

With peace, we hold no boundaries
in our world that can shield us from
the freedom of becoming human.

Be at peace with your own soul, then Heaven and Earth will be at peace with you.

ISAAC OF NINEVEH

Illuminate

Rejoice in your vision of love and
bring it out into the world,
embracing the spirit that seeks you
with grace.

Rejoice in the life you are given and
bring it into the world with every
breath of joy in being alive.

Rejoice in the compassion of your
heart and bring it out into the world
with the warmth of your human
spirit.

Rejoice in the light that burns the
darkness from your soul, and brings
it into the world by illuminating it
with your wisdom.

Rejoice in the time that will ferment
you with age and bring it into the
world with your humble reverence
for the wisdom of age.

Rejoice in your conscious awareness
of reality and bring it to the world
with self-awareness.

He is a wise man who does not grieve for the things which he has not, but rejoices for those which he has.

EPICTETUS

I Wait

I shall wait for your love to enter my
soul by leaving my doors open to
welcome the sweetness of your
coming fragrance.

I shall wait for the joy of my
existence by leaving my doors open
to hear the whisper of the coming
of age.

I shall wait for silence to enter my
ears by leaving my doors open to
listen for the sound of my mind that
holds me still.

I shall wait for the wisdom to make
me human by leaving my doors open
for truth to embrace my soul.

I shall wait for the light to enter the
darkness of my spirit by leaving my
doors open to see the beauty of your
glowing face.

I shall wait for fate to give me
direction by leaving my doors open
for my soul to move into the world.

The minute I heard my first love story, I started
looking for you, not knowing how blind
that was. Lovers don't finally meet
somewhere. They're in each
other all along.

RUMI

Spread Wide

Will we cast a net upon ourselves to
capture our souls in the moment of
our conscious perception of
becoming human?

Will we cast a net upon the world to
capture time in the moment of its
beginning?

Will we cast a net upon our reality to
capture our vision in the poetry of
our imagination?

Will we cast a net upon our mind to
capture our thoughts in the deep
ocean of our thinking?

Will we cast a net upon the one we
love to capture our lover in the pangs
of our hearts?

Will we cast a net upon our
happiness to capture the joy of living
in the beauty of our laughter?

Will we cast a net upon our fate to
capture the perception of reality that
moves our consciousness into the
world?

Do the difficult things while they are easy, and
do the great things while they are small.
A journey of a thousand miles
must begin with a single step.

LAO TZU

I Am Waiting

I will wait for love to enter my heart
the moment I open my soul to the
footsteps of her coming.

I will wait for the joy of my
existence when I open my spirit to
time as my most sacred guest.

I will wait for meaning to enter my
words as I open my eyes to the mind
that will bring me into
consciousness.

I will wait for the spirit to bring me
peace when I open myself to walking
out into the world to find myself.

I will wait for the light to enter my
eyes when I open my heart to the
darkness of my fears.

I will wait for the one who will make
me whole when I open my doors to
embrace my humble Self.

I will wait for silence to enter my
mind when I reflect on the wisdom
that voices my reality.

Nothing will make you happy until you choose to be happy. No person will make you happy unless you decide to be happy. Your happiness will not come to you. It can only come from you.

BUDDHA

Coming of Sorrow

The root of all pleasures is never to
let it grow into your soul, for the
moment it leaves, eternal sorrow for
its longing will torment your heart.

The root of happiness is to savor this
moment of joy, for the moment it
leaves, deep sorrow will cast over
your human spirit.

The root of power is never to let it
conquer your humanity; the moment
it leaves, no sorrow will come near
your mind.

The root of contentment is
acceptance of whatever you have;
the moment you are encircled by
greed, the veil of sorrow will cloud
your judgment.

The root of wealth is the health of
your being, for the moment it leaves,
growing sorrow will infect your
human existence.

The root of time is the life we grow
into the world; once it leaves,
withering sorrow will cast over our
aging faces.

If you can look into the seeds of time, and say which
grain will grow, and which will not,
speak then unto me.

WILLIAM SHAKESPEARE

Fear Me Not

Do not be afraid to take your first
step into a life of uncertainty, for the
moment you start to move, it will
unravel before your eyes.

Do not be afraid to speak against the
lies of this world, for the moment
you echo the truth, and all things will
unravel under the voice of your
wisdom.

Do not be afraid to love others, for
when you embrace their spirit, the
beauty of love will unfold in your
hearts.

Do not be afraid to look into the
darkness of your soul; the moment
you open your eyes, the beauty of
light will unravel the truth.

Do not be afraid to face the world's
hardships; when you are strong, your
burden of life will unravel with your
strength.

Do not be afraid to seek the mystical
nature of your being, for the moment
you seek knowledge, your
intelligence will unravel what you
desire to know.

You are only afraid if you are not in harmony with yourself.
People are afraid because they have never
owned up to themselves.

HERMANN HESSE

Wanting

Humans desire to live for eternity,
but they often lack the appetite for
simple living that comes with every
moment.

Humans desire the wealth of this
world, but can't hold it without
wasting it first on something more.

Humans desire to find love, but often
look for it in all the wrong places,
outside their hearts.

Humans desire a meaningful
existence, but often lack the moral
wisdom to discover their life's
purpose.

Humans desire the fruits of their
happiness, but don't know how to
enjoy them before the coming of age
takes them away.

Humans desire a world that they
can't have but will keep pursuing
until death takes it from them with
their final breath.

A man asked Gautama Buddha, "I want happiness."
Buddha said, First remove 'I,' that's EGO,
then remove "WANT," that's DESIRE.
See, now you are left with
only "HAPPINESS"

BUDDHA

Walk Away

You shall be healed the moment you
let go of the desires of this world and
walk away from them with no regret.

You shall be healed the moment you
detach yourself from the wealth of
this world and walk away empty-
handed with no anchors at your feet.

You shall be healed when you seek
the truth within yourself and walk
away into the world with wisdom
fully revealed.

You shall be healed when you
humble your pride to the will of time
and walk away into your fate with
humility in your mind.

You shall be healed when you realize
the uncertainty of life and walk away
seeking the all-revealing reality that
is here and now.

You shall be healed when you
forgive others who have done you
wrong and walk away with no
regrets from your human emotions.

"Detachment is not that you own nothing.
Detachment is that nothing owns you."

BHAGAVAD GITA

Chapter 2: Wisdom, Truth, Belief, and Faith

The wisdom of truth is in the faith that we come to believe. Truth can only be revealed when we open our minds to the wisdom it whispers to our souls. When we hold faith, truth will pave the way for us to walk upon and reach our life goals. Life's wisdom lies in our curiosity to know and remove the barriers between our inner and outer worlds, which are veiled in our conscious minds.

Truth has no value when we sell it for personal gain. Truth will hold no wisdom when we can't separate it from our illusions of reality. Truth is eternal, and humanity must defend it against the tyranny of evil. Wisdom is to become human when virtue teaches us to be righteous in our actions and deeds. Wisdom will humble our minds with the perception of time, molding our character and defining our will to be.

An honest soul will never deceive but will live for the integrity of faith in the wisdom of experience. The humanity of wisdom is the creed of civility and the moral foundation for a civilized nation. Wisdom is the collective spirit of our virtuous world that never bends to the will of power. The wisdom of faith is in the eyes of our inner storm and will shield us from the whirlwind of temptation. "Many Shades of Wisdom" are the many layers of truth written in our hearts and read by our minds with love and devotion.

When you believe it is your reality and your Faith is in your wisdom, then what you create in this world becomes your sanctuary in life.

SHAKOOR

Spirit of Wisdom

We only become human when we
strive to live and walk humbly on the
path that reveals the wisdom of our
existence.

The actions of our moral deeds will
emanate out into the world, guiding
humanity toward its ethical ways.

Will we leave our hearts open to
worldly reality and become the
guests of time in our mortal domain?

We become most thoughtful when
we continue to love the ones who
gave us a purpose for living.

We become reflective and
compassionate when we open our
minds to the spirit that gave us the
beauty of laughter, allowing it to
enter our consciousness.

We became the light of humanity
when we lifted the veil of darkness
from our eyes, revealing the truth of
reality reflected in our souls.

Happy are those who find wisdom . . . for her income is better than silver, and her revenue is better than gold. She is more precious than rubies; all of your goods cannot equal her.

JEWISH PROVERB

Spiritual Ground

We build our existence, brick by
brick, mortar by mortar, but nothing
can be erected without a spiritual
foundation.

We build our wisdom with every
moment, but without reflection, there
can be no wisdom in our vision.

We build our minds with conscious
awareness, but we will encounter
many obstacles if we navigate the
world with our eyes closed.

We build a love for humanity in
layers, but our selfish needs destroy
all we create in the heat of passion.

We build our dreams in the silence of
the night, but when we awaken, we
still face the reality of being human.

We build time with the hands of our
fate, and what we create is the legacy
of what we wish to become.

We build hope in times of
uncertainty to give us the faith to
guide our human will toward self-
realization.

Carefully watch your thoughts, for they become your words. Manage and watch your words, for they will become your actions. Consider and judge your actions, for they have become your habits. Acknowledge and watch your habits, for they shall become your values. Understand and embrace your values, for they become your destiny.

MAHATMA GANDHI

Speak Against

You saw me extend my spirit to
those in need, and now I extend my
soul to you, who needs you dearly.

You saw me walk out into the world
with open arms, and now I must
walk back home with slumbering
steps.

You saw me look at the world with
love and compassion, but they saw
me with wickedness and hateful
intentions from their hearts.

You saw me speak with wisdom in
my most trusted ways, but now they
speak against the truth with contempt
in their voice of reason.

You saw me with the courage to
fight for those who are weak, but
they gave me grief for my actions in
their most unjust ways.

You saw me struggle to uphold
human morality, but they
declared war on my moral character
with their destructive will.

Knock, then he'll open the door. Vanished, and he'll make you shine like the sun falls, and he'll raise you to the heavens. Become nothing, and he'll turn you into everything.

RUMI

We Reflect

The mirror will reflect what you see,
but you still want more of what you
don't see.

The mirror reflects the hidden truth
only when you cast a light upon
yourself by looking into it sincerely.

The mirror sees what lies within your
soul when your conscience seeks a
purpose that will define your life's
journey.

Hold up the mirror that reflects your
wisdom to the world so they can see
the whole vision of their humanity.

If you reflect the mirror upon the
sun, the light rays will bring your
shadow out of your hidden form.

Will you polish the mirror with your
own hands so that you can gaze into
the reality of your consciousness?

Why shatter the mirror that reflects
your true nature by fragmenting
yourself into a thousand pieces?

There are two ways of spreading light:
to be the candle or the
mirror that reflects it.

EDITH WHARTON

Seeking Curiosity

A curious spirit is never at rest; it is
always seeking when in search of
direction and purpose under its
conscious steps.

A curious mind can never stop
thinking of a more profound
understanding of the world and itself
when it reflects in silence on a
moonlit night.

A curious soul will seek unity in the
uncertainty of its existence and
search for the truth that will bind it to
humanity with searching eyes.

A curious body will lift the burden of
sorrow upon its shoulders until it can
offload itself from the world in
moments of reflection.

A curious voice will seek the words
that will bring the beauty of sound
into our hearts, the lyrics reflect a
poetic vision to our mystical mind.

A curious thought reflects on
wisdom written in time, molded by
the perception of age, etched on our
conscious mind.

If I see anything vital around me, it is precisely that spirit of adventure, which seems indestructible and is akin to curiosity.

MARIE CURIE

Be Aware

Guard against the thieves of this
world, for they will steal the wealth
hidden in your soul that you hold
most sacred.

Guard against the vanity in your
mind, for it will leave you weak in
your moral judgments when you
flaunt it to the world.

Guard against the evils of this world,
for they will take away your life with
no conscious afterthought.

Guard against the lies of this world,
for they will keep you blind and
ignorant of the vision in truth.

Guard against the disease of this
world, for it will infect your spirit
with the poison of hate, when you go
near it blindly.

Guard against the epiphany of chaos
spewed by this world by keeping faith
in time, and peace will settle it in the
temperament of your patience.

I laugh when I hear that the fish in the water is thirsty.
You don't grasp the fact that what is most alive of all
is inside your own house, and you walk from one
holy city to the next with a confused look! Kabir
will tell you the truth: go wherever you like, to
Calcutta or Tibet; if you can't find where your
soul is hidden, for you, the world
will never be real!

KABIR

Escape

Trapped in our conscious lives, we
can no longer escape from the web
of time that weaves in our hearts.

Trapped in our intellectual minds, we
can no longer think beyond the
abstract thoughts that encircle our
reasoning.

Trapped in worldly pleasures, we are
left empty, holding our hands out for
more when nothing but the wind is
left for us to embrace.

Trapped in our need for self-
realization, we can no longer see our
faces in the mirror of self-reflection.

Trapped in our mortal fate, we are
caught fighting against the will of
civilization with the voice of our
mind.

Trapped in the gravity of our world,
we no longer jump high enough to
seek and touch the sky.

Just as the ocean remains undisturbed by the incessant flow of water from rivers merging into it, likewise, the sage, who is unmoved despite the flow of desirable objects all around him attain peace, and not the person who strives to satisfy desires.

BHAGAVAD GITA

Trusting Self

If we believe in the courage of our
will, then we will achieve unity of
purpose in the time we have been
given.

If we believe in the truth of our faith,
then hardship will never bind us in
sorrow that hovers over us.

If we believe in the beauty of our
being, then the veil of consciousness
will reveal our true fate.

If we believe in the life we have been
given, our journey through time will
reveal our path into the world.

If we believe in hope for tomorrow,
then today will be the moment we
can borrow from eternity.

If we believe in our virtuous ways,
the truth will guide us toward our
righteous path in life.

If we believe in our dreams, we will
find a way to fulfill them by seeking
them in our worldly reality.

Trust in dreams, for in them is hidden the gate to eternity.

KHALIL GIBRAN

Moral Calm

Wisdom only comes when we face a
moral dilemma that challenges our
conscious mind to confront the
uncertainty of reality.

Our choices will determine our fate,
and the direction our lives will take
will determine our role in this world.

The storms of life will stir our inner
passions, and only courage can
weather the hardships that come with
ever-moving time.

Moral courage is the only power that
can stand up to the injustice of
human cruelty that comes to destroy
our humanity.

The most challenging path you take
in life will build your character and
give you the wisdom to define the
purpose of your existence.

A conflicted soul remains divided,
even when offered the most
straightforward path to resolution.

The heaviness of our footsteps will
become light when the spirit to move
carries them with the momentum of
our human curiosity.

Every experience, no matter how bad it seems,
holds within its blessing of some kind.
The goal is to find it.

BUDDHA

Wisdom Speaks

The voice of wisdom has spoken,
pointing us toward the path our
righteous steps can take in life.

The voice of wisdom opens our
minds to seek the truth that hides
under the veil of understanding.

The voice of wisdom settles in our
consciousness and awakens our
minds, guiding us toward the shores
of self-awareness.

The voice of wisdom touches our
hearts, breaking open the emotions
of love that seeps into our all-
embracing souls.

The voice of wisdom lifts our spirits
and gives us the freedom to
overcome the gravity that holds us
on the surface of our existence.

The voice of wisdom whispers to
humanity that we are guests of time,
the moment we come into this world.

Before you speak, let your words pass through three gates. At the first gate, ask yourself, "Is it true?" At the second gate, ask, "Is it necessary?" And at the third gate ask, "Is it kind?"

SUFI SAYING

They Say

You saw me extend my love to those
in need, and now I offer my heart to
you, who need me most.

You saw me come out into the world
with my feet, and now I must walk
back home with wayward steps.

You saw me look at the world with
love and compassion, but they saw
me with malice and hateful
intentions.

They saw me speak the truth in my
most honest ways, but now they
speak against the truth with
spite in their hearts.

They saw me take the courage to
defend those who were weak, but
they walked away from me when I
was mortally wounded.

They saw me bring light to those
who could not see, but they kept
their eyes closed and chose to remain
blind.

Whenever you argue with another wiser than yourself in order that others may admire your wisdom, they will discover your ignorance.

SAADI

Act of Deeds

If we abide by what we believe and
act through it, we have acquired the
will to live with freedom.

If we abide by the truth of what we
say and act truthfully, then we have
acquired the wisdom in our actions
to live morally.

If we abide by the courage to stand
against evil, then we have acquired
the strength to live for the good of
humanity.

If we abide by the rules of human
virtue, then we have acquired reason
to live mindfully in our conscious
existence.

If we abide by the fate of creation,
we have acquired a clear vision of
light in our life's journey with time.

If we abide by the movement of
time, we have acquired the will to
walk into the world with grace in our
steps.

If we abide by how we live, then the
imagination of our world will paint
our dreams in vivid colors.

A tree is known by its fruit; a man by his deeds.
A good deed is never lost; he who sows
courtesy reaps friendship, and he
who plants kindness gathers love.

SAINT BASIL

Elegant Mind

The elegance of fate can liberate
humanity from the compulsive
rituals of mundane existence.

The elegance of humility can walk us
on humble ground, moving us toward
the simplicity of life.

The elegance of a generous heart can
be there for those most in need when
life becomes most uncertain.

The elegance of your mind can
liberate you from heavy thoughts and
guide you toward the graceful form
of human intelligence.

The elegance of harmony can help
you grow into yourself and emerge
into the world with a strong moral
character.

The elegance of time in your
existence is the conscious moment
when you finally discover yourself at
the crossroads of life.

The elegance of love is to give
yourself to others and open your
heart to the one who will make you
complete.

Love is the crowning grace of humanity, the holiest right of the soul, the golden link which binds us to duty and truth, the redeeming principle that chiefly reconciles the heart to life, and is prophetic of eternal good.

PETRARCH

Act of Will

The will of your humanity is the will
to be human by striving toward the
perfection of your moral character in
the mold of time.

The will of your compassion is the
tender feelings you hold for others to
sacrifice yourself for the greater
good of humanity.

The will of your words is the lifting
spirit of your poetry that awakens
our consciousness to help us
reflect on the beauty of creation.

The will of moral courage is the
voice you hold consciously by
fighting for the truth against the
oppression of evil.

The will of your mind transcends
logic and gives you a reason to think
beyond the boundaries of your
human intelligence.

Your character will be the vision of
life that will define your fate the
moment you step into the world with
open eyes.

The will to win, the desire to succeed, the urge to reach your full potential . . . these are the keys that will unlock the door to personal excellence.

CONFUCIUS

Hidden Truth

Our eyes shall see the vision of truth
within our spirit as it emerges fully
revealed into the world.

Our eyes shall see the beauty of light
that manifests with the colors of
Nature, which becomes the subtle
shade of our sculptured vision.

Our eyes shall see the creative
imagination that brews in our minds,
manifesting in a poetic wave of
moving emotions that settle in our
consciousness.

Our eyes shall see the passion for
those we embrace with the never-
ending love we hold in our hearts.

Our eyes shall see the beauty of self-
reflection in the blurred lines of our
human imperfections.

Our eyes shall see the blindness of
our wayward ways, which keep us
from seeing our conscious light that
longs to touch our souls.

The human heart has hidden treasures, in secret kept, in silence sealed; The thoughts, the hopes, the dreams, the pleasures, whose charms were broken if revealed.

CHARLOTTE BRONTE

Selfless

Serve humanity with your heart; you
will gain their kindness and
boundless love.

Serve those in need, and you will be
praised for the humble act that will
bind you to humanity.

Serve yourself with the sincerity of
love, and you will cultivate a
friendship with your spirit in faith
and devotion.

Serve your worldly needs with
simplicity of action, and you will
gain time to reflect on your vision of
who you want to be.

Serve your mind with intelligence
and humility, and you will gain the
wisdom of life that will enrich your
imagination.

Serve your soul with virtuous deeds,
and you will receive the moral
compass to guide you on your long
journey through time.

Serve your purpose with your heart's
will, and you will achieve a
meaningful existence in
eternal time.

With faith, discipline, and selfless devotion to duty, there is nothing worthwhile that you cannot achieve.

MUHAMMAD ALI JINNAH

Instant In Time

In an instant, the mind can
encompass the infinity of our
imagination and return to the center
of our being, fully transformed.

Love can encompass our whole spirit
in one moment, only to be revered
when it walks away through our
heart's doors.

In one moment, we are born into the
wealth of our existence, only to be
treasured when we take our last
breath.

In one moment, consciousness
awakens us to the beauty of reality,
only to be realized when we become
lost in our dreams.

Time is held under the soles of our
feet in one moment, only to be
measured when we come to the end
of our journey.

In one moment, our mind builds
what the will desires, only to be
destroyed by the pursuit of power,
wealth, and fame.

In one moment, we come to know
ourselves, only to get lost when we
seek the illusions of the world that
distracts us from our truth.

You must live in the present, launch yourself on every wave, find your eternity in each moment.

HENRY DAVID THOREAU

Spirit of Salvation

It is through the redemption of our
humanity that we absolve ourselves
of the guilt inherent in being human
and regain our moral virtue.

There is no redemption for a soul
consumed in pleasure and seeking
salvation in its worldly wealth.

We are beyond redemption when we
are driven in our quest for power,
only to become powerless in the
lures that come to imprison our
souls.

Our only redemption is to give
ourselves to the world to free
ourselves from the human bondage
of our finite existence.

The voice of redemption whispers to
our hearts to give us the courage and
wisdom to let go of what we love
most.

The conscious redemption of our
human ways is to reflect inward and
walk outward, humbly, into our
willful minds, unbound by worldly
experience.

Three things are necessary for the salvation of man:
to know what he ought to believe; to know what
he ought to desire, and to know
what he ought to do.

SAINT THOMAS AQUINAS

All Is In You

In your words, thoughts transform
you into what your consciousness
wants you to become.

In your heart, love only enters when
you open the doors to the one who
knocks at your door.

In your vision, you realize yourself
only when you open your eyes to the
one who reflects reality in the mirror
of your mind's consciousness.

In your moments of silence, your
gaze is frozen upon the moving river
that flows deep into the ocean of
your soul.

In your truth, wisdom seeks you only
when virtue becomes your guiding
light that enters into your righteous
spirit.

In your life, you search for meaning
when time no longer gives you the
space to fulfill your purpose.

In your body, you house a world that
must live in harmony when you
nourish it with the spirit of discipline
and respect.

What lies behind you and what lies in front of you, pale in comparison to what lies inside of you.

RALPH WALDO EMERSON

Find Thyself

He who seeks wisdom in life shall
grow roots into their soul that longs
to become human.

He who finds himself shall know the
secrets of what one sees in their
inner reality, revealed by light.

He who seeks the light in darkness
shall reflect on the vision of what
one wants to see when one opens
one's eyes.

He who seeks the beauty of love
shall know why the heart suffers in
the fear of being broken.

He who seeks the purity of mind
shall transcend the universe of their
expanding imagination.

He who seeks harmony in the
mystical relationship with Nature
shall walk into the garden of roses to
breathe in the fragrance of life.

He who seeks the spiritual nature of
knowledge will humble themselves
to the limits of their understanding.

He who seeks does not find, but he who does not seek will be found.

FRANZ KAFKA

Consciousness

In the darkness of perception, the
mind is awakened by the reflection
of light that seeps into its conscious
eye.

In the perception of reality, the
conscious spirit is awakened by the
beauty of life that flirts with our
heart's emotions.

In the vision of love, the heart is
awakened by the whisper of the inner
voice, emanating from the depths of
our soul, to open its doors.

In the vastness of time, the conscious
mind remains still as we move
around with curiosity, seeking the
world.

In dialogue with our human nature,
we ask questions that bear no
answers and walk away with
reasoning that questions our motives.

In the wisdom of age, we realize that
children hold the most sacred virtues
we envy when we become too
human for the world.

I hope it is true that a man can die and yet not only live in others, but give them life, and not only life, but that great consciousness of life.

JACK KEROUAC

Worth Keeping

Desirable are those who take every
moment to relish the time given and
hold it with reverence, without
letting it go to waste.

Desirable moments are ingrained in
our minds and carry us through our
days and nights, allowing for
conscious reflection.

Desirable are those souls who never
relinquish their moral vision and
seek the wisdom that leads them to
self-realization.

Desirable are those who uphold
human freedom and carry the light of
humanity to unmask the darkness of
human nature.

Desirable are those who find love in
their spirit and carry it into the world
with the power of persuasion.

Desirable are those who lead us by
example, and take responsibility for
their shortcomings.

Morality is not the doctrine of how we may make ourselves happy, but how we may make ourselves worthy of happiness.

IMMANUEL KANT

The Self Inside

I am the shadow within your light to
give you the wisdom to see the
darkness of your wayward path.

I am the beginning that moves
toward your end, said the soul to
your wayward steps.

I am the words that linger under your
voice, said the mind to your
wayward consciousness.

I am the love that burns in your
wholesome world, said the
smoldering emotions to your
wayward heart.

I am all in your world of
nothingness, said time to your
wayward existence.

I am the intellect in your human
logic, said experience to your
wayward intelligence.

I am the truth in your illusions of
reality, said wisdom to your
wayward mind.

If you are vigilant and make a stern effort to reject every thought when it rises, you will soon find that you are going deeper and deeper into your own inner self, where there is no need for your effort to reject the thoughts.

RAMANA MAHARSHI

Whom To Call

Whom shall we call when we have
lost the ways of our existence and
wander in all directions, searching
for the light of purpose?

Whom shall we see when the wide-
open eyes only see the dark vision of
our human nature?

Whom shall we listen to when
silence becomes the loudest voice no
one listens to?

Whom shall we recall when the
wilderness of civilization has
become a desolate wasteland of lost
souls?

Whom shall we love when our hearts
drown in the watershed emotions
that overwhelm our human spirit?

Whom shall we embrace when the
hands of time have taken us too far
into the world?

Whom shall we seek that will inspire
us beyond our limits and lift our
imagination to reach for the stars?

Whom shall I call on? Who will share with me the
wretched happiness of staying alive?

SERGEI YESENIN

Find the Will

We seek our wisdom through time
only when we become conscious of
our mind's need to capture
experience with our creative
imagination.

We seek our truth through silent
reflection, speaking to our hearts
with love and compassion.

We build our dreams through our
vision of creation only when the will
to bring them to life becomes our
sole purpose.

We seek our spirit through suffering
only when we sacrifice our human
nature for spiritual salvation.

We seek our fate with every shade of
reality to find the vision that fulfills
our purpose in life.

We seek the one who knows us well,
only to realize that it lives within our
souls with peace and tranquility.

Peace comes from within. Do not seek it without.

BUDDHA

Mirror of Reflection

Through reflection, we see the world
in all its forms, reflected to us with
the wisdom of life.

Through reflection, we can touch the
boundaries of truth that reflect to us
with conscious morality.

Through reflection, we seek a
journey that mirrors our will and
reflects us as time passes.

Through reflection, we find silence
holding us back from the world,
which reflects on us through the
symphony of sound.

Through reflection, we carry the
burden of life within our minds,
which reflects us with the spirit of
freedom.

Through reflection, we meditate by
listening to our breath, which reflects
us with the air we breathe.

Through reflection, we come to
terms with our finite existence by
accepting our fate in humble times.

The world is a looking glass and gives back to every man the reflection of his own face.

WILLIAM MAKEPEACE THACKERAY

Don't Move

Be still in your thoughts; all things
will come to your mind with the
conscious grace of self-reflection.

Be still in your faith, and the world
will become the center of your being
when you believe in yourself.

Be still in your vision; the light will
enter your eyes, bringing many
shades to your perception of reality.

Be still in your silence, and wisdom
will reveal the essence of your
mindfulness to your conscious Self.

Be still in your steps; time will
journey through your life with the
wisdom of age, weathered by
worldly experience.

Be still in your meditative state
under the breath of your existence,
and you will feel the essence of your
mysticism imbued in deep
sentiments.

You do not need to leave your room. Remain sitting at your table and listen. Do not even listen, simply wait, be quiet, still, and solitary. The world will freely offer itself to you to be unmasked; it has no choice; it will roll in ecstasy at your feet.

FRANZ KAFKA

I believe

Those who keep faith in tomorrow
will live for today in their most
truthful ways.

Those who keep faith in life will live
their lives in the most timely ways.

Those who keep faith in truth will
become conscious of their morality
in their most spiritual ways.

Those who keep faith in a better
world will fight for justice in their
most just ways.

Those who keep faith in humanity
will give the world wisdom in their
most human ways.

Those who keep faith in a better
tomorrow will find what they need to
move forward in their momentous
way.

Those who keep faith burning will
find the fire that will give them the
light that will show them the way.

Faith is an oasis in the heart that will never be reached by the caravan of thinking.

KHALIL GIBRAN

Light Reveals

The light has released the shadow of
our existence; is it walking toward us
or away from our human form?

The shadow of our dreams has
surrendered its will to the night; will
it bring us back to reality or moves
us further into our dreams?

The shadow of our perception has
drowned us in our minds; will our
thoughts surface, or sink deeper into
our consciousness?

The shadow of time casts the path in
rays of light upon us; will we realize
it before our end, or continue to walk
in our wayward journey?

The shadow of darkness hides us in
our fear of uncertainty; will we be
able to escape from its grip, or will it
imprison us in its walls of doubt?

The shadow of our suffering
humbles us to the ground; will we be
able to lift our spirits or crumble
under the weight of our existence?

Every man casts a shadow; not his body only, but his imperfectly
mingled spirit. This is his grief. Let him turn
which way he will, it falls opposite the sun;
short at noon, long at eve.
Did you never see it?

HENRY DAVID THOREAU

With Time

What has happened becomes the
mold for our conscious mind, etched
in the clay of our watery existence.

What will happen is realized only as
we walk through time, paving the
road toward tomorrow we seek for
ourselves today.

What will happen awaits us with
great expectations when we remain
calm, waiting for it to come
knocking at our doors.

What will happen is written in
human history and is bound to be
repeated when we fail to learn from
the past that defines us today.

What is going to happen will happen
when the nature of life and death is
determined by the fate of time.

What has happened becomes a
lesson for humanity, and what will
happen becomes the voice of
wisdom for tomorrow.

Magic is believing in yourself, if you can do that you can make anything happen.

JOHANN WOLFGANG VON GOETHE

Silence Speaks

Silence will reflect in our words, and
wisdom will come into our minds
awareness with the voice of sincerity.

Silence will hold us still in a life that
moves all around in the vast stream
of time and space.

Silence will hold us firm to our faith
as the world's uncertainty looms over
us like a shadow in the dimness of
light.

Silence will reflect in our souls as
the vision of reality reveals us to
ourselves in the conscious truth of
our human existence.

Silence will enter our hearts as the
love of life whispers to our spirit,
opening our doors to the one who
will make us whole.

Silence will lift the veil of darkness
and reveal the true beauty of our
enlightened mind.

The water in a vessel is sparkling; the water in the sea is dark.
The small truth has words which are clear;
the great truth has great silence.

RABINDRANATH TAGORE

I Know Not

Humility will come when you climb
the highest mountain, only to realize
that you must quickly come down
fast to breathe the air of sustenance.

Humility will come when you seek
knowledge and realize the vastness
of your imagination can never be
known.

Humility will come when time walks
away from our souls as old age
realizes its fading youth.

Humility will come when great
suffering becomes a tsunami of
overwhelming emotions that pulls us
in, as we realize the fragility of our
human existence.

The humility of our humble ways
will guide our steps as we realize the
never-ending path our lives must
walk.

Humility will walk away from our
pride by seeking the path that covers
the nakedness of our human nature.

To know that we know what we know, and to know that we do not know what we do not know that is true knowledge.

NICOLAUS COPERNICUS

Human Will

Stand firm in your thoughts, and you
will never fall deep into doubt about
your uncertain existence.

Stand firm in the storms of your
worldly ways; you will see it calmly
settle in your conscious mind.

Stand firm in your fast-paced life,
and you will find time to smell the
fragrance of Nature's beauty in your
garden of roses.

Stand firm in the flux of your
emotions, and you will find the
wisdom to make peace with your
loving Self.

Stand firm in your journey through
time, and you will find the path of
meaningful existence revealed to
your inner eye.

Stand firm against the tyranny of
evil, and you will find the fire of
morality burning with human virtues.

A man dies when he refuses to stand up for that which is right. A man dies when he refuses to stand up for justice. A man dies when he refuses to take a stand for that which is true.

MARTIN LUTHER KING, JR.

Humble Life

The strength of your character is to
let go of human pleasures and seek
the simplicity of life in your worldly
ways.

The strength of your character lies in
humbling yourself and striving to
live humbly in your humble ways.

The strength of your character is to
walk with momentum in your
footsteps and travel through time in
meaningful ways.

The strength of your character is to
gain wisdom through your deeds and
give hope to those in need with your
giving ways.

The strength of your character is to
uphold dignity and give your spirit
the courage to fight for freedom in
your mortal ways.

The strength of your character will
weather the storms of doubt and give
your mind the temperament to
remain calm in your momentous
ways.

Out of suffering have emerged the strongest souls;
the most massive characters are
seared with scars.

KHALIL GIBRAN

See Within

He who lives inside your soul has a
more extraordinary role than the
world you create outside your doors.

He who is your inner voice speaks
the greater truth than the voice that
stirs your emotions from outside
your doors.

He who is born inside you grows
greater in wisdom than the one who
experiences the world from outside
your doors.

He who looks inside of you sees
your true Self, more than the one
who sees you from outside your
doors.

He who hides inside you is a greater
threat to your peace than the enemy
that lurks outside your doors.

He who searches for inner meaning
sees their purpose more clearly than
the one who voices their teaching
from outside their doors.

Everyone rushes elsewhere and into the future, because no one wants to face one's own inner self.

MICHEL DE MONTAIGNE

I Know You

The wisdom of learning is to unlearn
what you have learned so you can
learn something more the next day.

The wisdom of knowledge is the
intelligence to realize that the more
you seek, the less you will come to
know.

The wisdom of life is to do more
with time than to live long in time.

The wisdom of self-determination is
to break free from yourself, rather
than imprisoning yourself within
your walls in the name of freedom.

The wisdom of your mind will never
fragment your thoughts, but will
gather them with perception to make
your reasoning whole.

The wisdom of time is to capture the
moment in your consciousness rather
than letting it escape from your
awareness.

To know is to know that you know nothing. That is the meaning of true knowledge.

SOCRATES

Cast Thy Light

The shades of wisdom are layered in
time, coloring our reality with the
poetic brush of our imagination.

The shades of truth slip into our
consciousness, and the spirit reflects
on them with a poetic expression of
our humanity.

The shades of light reveal the hidden
reality of creation to our eyes and
bring it into realization through its
poetic beauty.

The shades of love flow into our
mystical emotions; we can only feel
them once we embrace them with
our poetic mind.

The shades of our existence are
etched in time, and the water in our
clay becomes our poetic soul.

The shades of time become the
mosaic of our civilization, and the
fragments of our history become our
poetic story.

At times, our own light goes out and is rekindled by a spark from another person. Each of us has cause to think with deep gratitude of those who have lighted the flame within us.

ALBERT SCHWEITZER

Voice of Silence

The sound of silence is what our
minds hear most, but the voice of
wisdom will never remain quiet.

The sound of laughter makes the soul
dance, but the rhythm of life is no
longer the world's music.

The sound of an echo brings us back
to life, but the time reflected in our
youth is no longer visible on our
faces.

The sound of birds at the dawn of
light awakens our consciousness, but
the lingering perception of our
dreams will not be heard outside our
windows.

The sound of our beating hearts
moves our spirits to run free, but we
easily fall into the web of love's
charm.

The world's reality colors our
emotions, but what we see does not
filter into our consciousness.

Listen to the secret sound, the real sound, which is inside you. The one no one talks of speaks the secret sound to himself, and he is the one who has made it all.

KABIR

Chapter 3: Love, Beauty, Heart, and Friendship

Love is all-revealing when the beauty of our hearts shines upon the world with warmth and compassion. The wisdom of love breaks open our souls to let in the light, washing away our many shades of imperfections. In love, we become humane, and through love we become human. Love can only enter our souls when we accept ourselves as we are, not who we want to be. Love can only be realized when we do not fear surrendering ourselves to the one we love.

Nature's beauty is divine love given to us, accompanied by a spiritual awareness of the miracle of creation. The world's beauty is reflected in our eyes when we find the vision that colors our conscious imagination. The beauty of our thoughts becomes poetic when the name of the beloved is written in our souls. The wings of freedom lift love to touch us in our dreams under the star-filled night. The burning emotions brew in our hearts, and the fire that love creates will smolder with passion, heaving in our spirits.

Love will awaken our conscious mind and give us the purpose to walk out into the world to find ourselves. There is only solace in the warmth of a candle's light that glows in the beauty of love; our eyes long to see.

Love is eternal when we seek it with our souls from beginning to end. Love is never true when we yearn for it with a passion that destroys the subtle beauty of its charm. The Many Shades of Wisdom will dissolve love into our emotions, imbued with life's fragrance, leaving us breathless when we chase it with our whole existence.

A heart can never be broken when it is given love.
It can only shatter all the barriers
to love that you create.

SHAKOOR

Love Gives

What will they say when the soul
falls in love with you, and the eyes
of the world becomes envious of
your love affair?

Your faithful friend lurks within you,
and the wisdom of two as one is
divine in love's greatness.

What can a river give to the ocean
but a thirst for unity that longs to be
fulfilled by the will of love?

As we gather our beauty in conscious
love, we become the mosaic of our
vision in each other's eyes.

We are lured into love that burns us
with emotions and consumes us in
passion when light touches the soul.

A loving heart will wait for you in
silence as wandering eyes seek your
beauty that emerges from the depth
of shimmering light.

Even after all this time, the sun never says to the earth, "you owe me." Look what happens with a love like that. It lights up the whole sky.

HAFEZ

There, I Was

I am like a river that seeks your
water; seek me as your great ocean
that flows into the depth of your soul.

I am the deep spirit that awakens
your mind when you emerge from
within yourself.

I am the love that will grow roots in
your soul when you water my spirit
with your passionate hands.

I am the light that will wash away
the darkness from your eyes when
you light the candle with your
conscious love.

I am the joy that will lift away your
worldly sorrow the moment you give
your burden for me to carry.

I am the fire that will burn your
humanity into the ashes of my
smoldering passions when you come
near me with your glowing heart.

I am the shadow in your form; see
how I bring you into the light with
one spark of inspiration.

I am I, and you are you, but through
me, you will become all you want to
be when we become the one with
wholeness of love.

Love, you are my certainty. Lift me to the
stars. This "I" is a figment of
my imagination.

RUMI

Walk The Path

The empathy of kindness is the light
that emanates from your soul to
bring you into harmony with the
world.

Will you trust me unequivocally,
take my hand, and walk with me on
our destined path into eternity?

We become human when we give
our hearts the purpose of seeking the
love that will grow roots in our
being.

The open door into our worldly
existence becomes our way of
moving through time and space with
rhythm in our steps.

We become most sympathetic when
we continue to love the ones who
gave us the purpose to live a
meaningful existence.

We become wise with compassion
when we open our spirit to the one
who gave us the beauty of laughter
to dance with joy in our hearts.

No one saves us but ourselves. No one can and no one may. We ourselves must walk the path.

BUDDHA

Wandering

The power of love binds us in the unity of our spirit, moving us toward the greater whole with grace in our steps.

A river wanders in all directions and can only find unity toward the depth of the great ocean when lured in by love's mystical pull.

Humanity will wander in all directions, seeking the essence of life, but unity of purpose and meaning will come when both are realized.

The unity of our existence is layered in time, and the footsteps of our journey are often left behind.

Will we lie still in time to seek unity in consciousness that marvels at the mystical nature of our existence?

The unity of our vision is the truth of reality, reflected in the light of our conscious being when we awaken from our dreams.

Wandering into ourselves is our spiritual journey, but finding ourselves becomes our life's purpose.

To the mind that is still, the whole universe surrenders.

LAO TZU

Self-realization

Great compassion will extend its
hands to you; take it and embrace it
with your heart and soul before it
walks away.

The soul of creation is the beauty of
life, and the moment we are born, we
strive to live to the fullest, immersed
in the time we are given.

The vision of our humanity is
imbued with love and compassion
the moment we embrace the joy and
sorrow of others with our hearts.

Life's journey is our moment of self-
realization, cherishing the wealth of
time spent wisely without wasting a
day.

Give up the world, and you shall
gain your freedom, but chase the
world, and you become a slave to
your nature, shackled by your will.

The spirit of love echoes in Nature's
calling for our souls, but we do not
hear it and continue chasing the
sound of worldly noise.

Knowledge of the self is the mother of all knowledge.
So, it is incumbent on me to know my Self, to know it completely,
to know its minutiae, its characteristics,
its subtleties, and its very atoms.

KHALIL GIBRAN

I In You

I have created you in my image, so
you can reflect on yourself through
me with the vision of your world.

I have created you in the wisdom of
light so you can see me through the
darkness in your soul with many shades
of color.

I have created you in the love of my
spirit so you can walk through my
path on the landscape of time.

I have created you in Nature's beauty
so that you can embrace me through
the love that emanates to illuminate
the world.

I have created you with strong hands
of freedom; I shall set you free from
this world with no attachments to
your worldly needs.

I have created you with sincerity, so
you can remember me through the
words of wisdom I sealed in your
soul.

Nothing great is created suddenly, any more than a bunch of grapes or a fig. If you tell me that you desire a fig. I answer you that there must be time. Let it first blossom, then bear fruit, then ripen.

EPICTETUS

In Love

Love will bind our spirit to the one
we love and take us on our mystical
journey to seek the one we love.

Love is the only emotion that gives
our lives the beauty of purpose,
allowing us to feel fulfillment and
joy, and to embrace our lives with
serenity.

Love is the light that overshadows all
darkness, giving us the vision of
reality, a vision we see in many
shades of beauty.

Love is the voice that brings music
to our hearts and makes our spirits
dance in harmony with time.

Love is the breath of willful
existence and the air that holds us in
ecstasy the moment we breathe it in
with our conscious mind.

Love is the universe that
encompasses us all in the majesty of
our existence and gives us reason to
keep on living.

Love knows no difference between life
and Death. The one who gives you
a reason to live is also the one who
takes your breath away

MIRZA GHALIB

One Within

A friend will love you with the
warmth of her heart, but an enemy
will love you with a heart of envy.

A friend will provide you with
everything you want, but an enemy
will take what you need most and
leave you empty.

A friend will suffer with you when
you suffer most, but an enemy will
make you suffer when he suffers
least.

A friend will give your soul the gift
of laughter, but an enemy will keep
you crying in your tears of sorrow.

A friend will reveal to you the beauty
of life, but an enemy will take away
the mystical purpose of your
existence.

A friend will open her heart in time
of need, but an enemy will lure you
into their trap with the intent to
destroy.

If I could take your troubles, I would toss them into the sea, but all
these things I'm finding are impossible for me.
I cannot build a mountain or catch a rainbow fair,
but let me be what I know best,
a friend who is always there.

KHALIL GIBRAN

Selfless Love

You shall love others as you love
yourself when you give up the
attachments to your human desires.

You shall love others as you love
yourself when you erase the
boundaries between I and They.

You shall love others as you love
yourself when you let love embrace
your inner Self.

You shall love others as you love
yourself, the moment you bring
compassion into the darkness of
your soul.

You shall love others as you love
yourself when you lift the mask of
hypocrisy that hides your real face.

You shall love others as you love
yourself, the moment you look into
the mirror of self-reflection to see
yourself.

You shall love others as you love
yourself when you seek the truth in
the wisdom of your human ways.

He who has no attachments can love others, for his love is pure and divine. And it is from those small acts of love that you truly can be happy.

BHAGAVAD GITA

I Love You

When I found the direction of my
fate under the soles of her feet, I
moved away from my being toward
her love with my silent steps.

When I found her waiting for me for
a thousand years, I came to her door
with my life in my hands for a
moment of her eternity.

When I found the beauty of life
reflected in her eyes, I gave her the
love of my heart for the joy of her
spirit.

When I felt the warmth of her smile
touch my eyes, I held her close to my
vision, never to let her part from my
loving embrace.

When I found the voice of her words
awakening my conscious mind, she
made me a poet in my mystical
longing.

When I found the purpose of my
existence in her world, she gave me a
home to rest my weary soul.

When I found that her name was
written in my fate, I searched for her
in my dreams, etched in the beauty
of a star-filled night.

The sun has set, its flush only is left. I will give my life for a glimpse of you. My fault, I did not know that your love has made me dance tonight like mad.

BULLEH SHAH

I Am Offering

In the spirit of friendship, our hearts
will offer the sentiments of humanity
to the ones we love.

A true friend will love us faithfully
and be at our door when we need
them most.

There are no judgments or equals
among friends in the cold and
heartless world surrounding our
existence.

The world's treasures may hold
value, but the wealth in friendship is
most precious to the soul of
humanity.

Blessed is the spirit that opens its
doors to the friend who will give it
back what it has lost in the world.

The eternal bond of friendship will
remain sacred throughout the human
experience and can never be broken
by the bending will of this world.

Bless the friend who brings solace
and light to your soul in moments of
darkness and uncertainty that may
come with time.

One of the most beautiful qualities of true friendship is to understand and to be understood.

SENECA

Vision To See

A wounded pride bears the scars of
vanity and will take a lifetime to
heal.

A joyful life can bear the burden of
time and walk you through your
inner storms with the stillness of
mind.

A wise person can find wisdom in
the simplest things, and will not
carry the burden of pride.

A curious mind can see beyond the
reality of this world and search for
meaning with conscious reflection.

A beautiful spirit can see the
mystical love that binds them to the
heart of their human nature with their
true Self.

A loving heart knows how to change
the world through acts of kindness
and compassion toward humanity.

A vision of light reveals the many
shades of reality, reflecting the
colors of the world in our eyes.

I can do things you cannot, you can do things I cannot;
together, we can do great things.

MOTHER TERESA

Show Me

Will you teach me to love humanity
unconditionally before my heart
breaks into question and doubts?

Will you show me the way into your
soul before I leave this world
through your doors?

Will you show me the vision of your
beauty before my love blinds me
with emotions that will not let me
enter your heart?

Will you help me find myself before
I am lost in the world, searching for
your love on this endless road toward
life?

Will you walk with me to the end of
my journey before I part from your
heart in the fragments of time?

Would you light the sacred lamp
before I bow to the light to embrace
your shadow with my loving form?

Will you offer me your soul and take
the one that the world has given me
to fill this emptiness with the
compassion of your love.

You have to grow from the inside out. None can teach you; none can make you spiritual. There is no other teacher but your own soul.

SWAMI VIVEKANANDA

Awakened

Day and night, we long to live in the
beauty and tranquility of our human
nature, only to wake up restless,
chasing dreams.

Night and day, we envision a world
filled with the majestic colors
painted on the canvas of our
imagination, only to wake up
searching for the light in our
conscious mind.

Time and day, we hope to take in the
fragrance of life that emanates from
our spirit, only to wake up wanting
more time to breathe.

At a specific time of day, we feel the
rhythm of our being, which beats in
our hearts, only to wake up
heartbroken when the feeling fades.

In this age of time, we know we have
lived and shall live in every moment,
only to wake up fearing that our end
will come tomorrow.

Day and night, we walk seeking the
purpose for our existence, only to
wake up lost in our ways with no
path in sight.

Perseverance is a great element of success. If you only knock long enough and loud enough at the gate, you are sure to wake up somebody.

HENRY WADSWORTH LONGFELLOW

Love Awoke

Your love awakened me, the sole
purpose of my existence, when you
let me enter your soul.

I was awakened from my dreams the
moment you became my reality, and
I was consumed by your vision,
which burned with passion with your
love.

I was awakened into my conscious
mind when I realized that you were
the only one who would embrace me
with the warmth of your love.

I was awakened by a heart that
whispered your name, and I realized
you had mesmerized me the moment
I saw you appear in my mystical
eyes.

I was awakened by the sound of the
summer breeze and the scent of your
fragrance, which moved my senses
with your luring beauty.

I was awakened by the silent steps
knocking at my door, which
saddened me when I realized they
were not yours.

They say love opens a door from one heart to another. But if there is no wall, how can there be a door?

RUMI

Self-giving

It is in the compassion of our being
that we become most empathetic to
comfort those who need us most.

It is with compassion that we learn to
forgive and empathize with those
who love us the least.

We give ourselves compassion for
the betterment of humanity, to give
rather than receive from others, and
to fulfill their hearts.

We all become one with compassion
when we give the world hope of a
better day through empathy and
kindness.

It is with compassion that we extend
our hand to the one in need and
embrace them with our whole being.

It is with compassion that our spirit
is born and moves out into the world
with the majesty of peace and
harmony.

Love and compassion are necessities, not luxuries.
Without them, humanity cannot survive.

DALAI LAMA

Blinding Love

Love will bind your spirit to the one
you love and walk you toward the
path for the one you seek.

Love is the mystical emotion that
gives your life the beauty of
fulfillment, allowing you to savor
your soulful existence in every
moment of time.

Love is the light that overcomes all
darkness and becomes the vision of
reality that all will come to see.

Love is the voice that brings music
to your soul and awakens your spirit
to dance in the ecstasy of life.

Love is the breath of conscious
mystery, the air that holds you in
your embrace when you breathe it
with mystical joy.

Love is your seeking spirit that will
find you when binding love erases all
barriers between two souls.

Your task is not to seek love, but merely to seek and find all the barriers within yourself that you have built against it.

RUMI

I Am Close

In my presence, you will hear me
with my loving voice, said the mind
to your bewildered soul.

I will embrace you with complete
love of my being, said the spirit in
part to your wandering mind.

In my presence, you will walk out of
this cave of darkness, said the light
to our wisdom, anticipating your
coming vision.

In my presence, you will hold no
moral ground, said the hand of
justice to the will of evil.

In my presence, age will remain
eternally bound to time, said life to
the coming of death.

In my presence, love will remain
sincere with devotion, said the heart
to your all-embracing spirit.

In my presence, you are the guest in
my home, said the world to the
beginning of your life's journey.

When you love someone, the best thing you can offer is your presence. How can you love if you are not there?

THICH NHAT HANH

Uplifting Spirit

We stand before our doors to
welcome humanity into our hearts
and give them the candor of love
from our souls.

We stand before our eyes to see the
beauty of life as a vision of time
molded by the hands of creation.

We stand on our feet to walk toward
our end, willfully leaving our steps
behind for our life to remember.

We stand before our love, feeling our
passion awakened in our hearts,
emotions we can embrace.

We stand before the world to become
the beacon of light and erase the
darkness of our human ways.

We stand before time, aged by the
wisdom layered in the dust of time
for the wind to sweep it away.

He who would learn to fly one day must first learn to stand and walk and run and climb and dance; one cannot fly into flying.

FRIEDRICH NIETZSCHE

Silent Reflection

The beauty of the Self will be
revealed the moment you look in the
mirror of self-reflection.

The beauty of your words will be
known the moment you voice them
with your passion for truth in your
wisdom.

The beauty of your will comes to be
realized when you walk out into the
world with curiosity to seek the
devotion of Nature's offerings.

The beauty of your moral virtues will
lead you out of blindness when you
open your mind to seek yourself.

The beauty of your human spirit
reveals your character when
humanity embraces its imperfections
with humility.

The beauty of love enters your heart
when you bow to it with the
surrender of your human will.

The beauty of silence speaks
volumes when you reflect on it with
your silent mind.

When the whole world is silent, even one voice becomes powerful.

MALALA YOUSAFZAI

Love Fulfills

Let us find love in our hearts so we
can grow into ourselves and blossom
within the fragrance of our
happiness.

Let us find love for each other as our
destinies are meant to be; walking
toward the bridge to love is where
we meet.

Let us love each other for all
eternity; this moment is ours in
totality, and the next moment is love
supreme.

Let us love each other
unconditionally, for we are like two
drifting clouds in the wind encircling
the majestic, purple mountains under
our spacious sky.

Let us grow roots in love, for love's
mystical light will glow above and
beyond darkness, reflecting in each
others' eyes.

Let us journey through time hand in
hand, seeking each other with love to
fulfill life's most cherished moments.

Let us seek the Self that loves us the
most in a world that is envious of our
unity with each other.

Let love lead your soul. Make it a place to
retire to a kind of cave, a retreat
for the deep core of being.

ATTAR OF NISHAPUR

I Am Born

The day you are born is when you
begin to live, growing into time and
flourishing in the beauty of your
emerging world.

The day you open your eyes is when
light enters the window of your soul,
coloring your vision with shades of
mystical wonder.

The day you are awakened into
consciousness, you begin seeking
yourself in the vastness of your
mind's imagination.

The day you learn to speak is when
you begin to write your poetry of
life, expressed on the canvas of your
conscious mind.

The day you take your first step
marks the beginning of your journey
forward in time, leading you to
complete it from start to finish.

The day you sell your soul is when
you lose your humanity to the allure
of this world, you will never regain it.

Don't judge each day by the harvest you reap, but by the seeds that you plant.

ROBERT LOUIS STEVENSON

Words I Say

Every word I say speaks of your love
as it grows in my heart to emanate
into your world, fully revealed.

Every word I whisper to you is
poetic love, full of sincerity as it
parts my lips to seek and touch your
loving soul.

Every word that enters my mind is a
fragment of your existence as it
settles into my mystical thoughts,
forming a mosaic of my life's vision.

Every word I write lingers upon my
pen as it strokes the emotions that
become the verses of hidden
meaning written on my empty
dreams.

Every word is lifted from my
worldly wisdom as I walk into my
journey to write the story of my life
through your being.

Every word sheds light on your
human mind, which reveals subtle
shades of your inner nature to the
world that houses your love.

One word frees us of all the weight and
pain in life. That word is love.

SOPHOCLES

Spirit of Love

In spirit so loved, we are bound to
our loving emotions to seek the
world in its most precious moments,
so dear to our hearts.

In time so loved, we age through our
experience to gain wisdom that takes
us far into life's journey.

In life, so loved, we breathe in the
joy of living and breathe out the
memories of our past, which we have
forgotten.

In eyes so loved, we look out into the
beauty of Nature to see the colors of
light that settles on our conscious
vision.

In mystical poetry so loved, we voice
our needs for the one who touched
our soul with the warmth of their
charming gaze.

In beauty so loved, we chase the
wind imbued with the fragrance of
life that emanates from within.

We love life, not because we are used to living
but because we are used to loving.

FRIEDRICH NIETZSCHE

Loving Soul

I shall love you a thousand times, in
a thousand ways, which makes love
seen in fragments of a thousand
dreams.

I shall love you as I love myself
when your spirit erases all
hindrances between the body and
soul.

I shall love you with my soulful eyes
the moment you become the vision
of reality under the beauty of a star-
glazed dream.

I shall love you with my tender
emotions when the warmth of my
lips touches the softness of your rosy
cheeks.

I shall love you like no other the
moment I give myself to you and no
one else.

I shall love you like the wind that
holds life's fragrance emanating from
your soul, heaving under my breath.

I shall love you the moment you
come my way, as my eyes reflect on
you with mystical stillness in my
gaze.

Blessed is the influence of one true loving,
human soul on another.

GEORGE ELIOT

Rejoiced

When we saw your spirit's moral
deeds, we all rejoiced in your
sacrifice for the good of humanity.

When we saw the love you held
inside your heart, we rejoiced when
you opened your doors to welcome
all who wished to come in.

When we heard the words of wisdom
whispered from your lips, we
rejoiced in the truth you gave our
ailing spirits.

When we saw the beauty of your
face, we rejoiced in the light that
glowed from your eyes within.

When we felt the strength of your
character, we rejoiced in the spirit of
your soulful presence.

When we saw the grace in your
human ways, we rejoiced at the
shining virtue of your enlightened
mind.

When we heard the wisdom of your
life, we rejoiced in the lessons you
instilled in our hearts.

He is a wise man who does not grieve for the things which he has not, but rejoices for those which he has.

EPICTETUS

Chapter 4: Life, Death, Journey, and Time

The journey through time is layered between life and death. The road we take in the world will determine the fate of our existence. To live is to love life, and to let go of yourself is to embrace every moment that comes your way. Death is an illusion embedded in our fears, but not living is dying within yourself while still living. Only life is our ultimate reality and the most sacred possession given to our souls. If we don't live life, then we die a thousand deaths. If we don't value time, we grow old, and our every moment is wasted with our withering youth.

The human spirit will never know its destined path until it shines a light upon itself. Life is a dream for those who live too big or too small in their fast-paced perception of the world. The wisdom of life is to become conscious of every minute that time gives and hold it with value before it slips away. The beginning and end hold us, prisoners, when we chase the lures of pleasures that consume us completely.

We begin to envision life when we become conscious and ponder the uniqueness of our creative spirit. We are guests in eternal time, and none are here to stay. Life becomes most precious near our end, and we take time for granted as we race through our youth. Time is most beautiful when we overcome our suffering and carry our burdens with the strength of will. Life is most precious when we find our purpose and fall in love with the beauty of our dream-like world. The vision of life is the mosaic of our existence, the fragments of our journey that we take with our mortal steps. "Many Shades of Wisdom" are revealed through time as we grow into ourselves with every breath of life in our souls.

Our existence in this world is wasted
if we journey through time, wandering
with no direction, chasing
empty dreams that
hold no value.

SHAKOOR

Oh, Life!

Oh, Life, where is the holy water that
will wash away our blind rituals and
give us a new beginning to cleanse
ourselves?

Oh, Life, why do we build walls
around our hearts that only imprison
us in the faith that houses our spirit?

Oh, Life, how do we walk away
from the world that no longer holds
us above ground?

Oh, Life, what is this question we
keep asking the soul when we can't
find the answer to our purpose in the
world?

Oh, Life, who will tell us that
temples, mosques, and synagogues
no longer exist within the Self?

Oh, Life, are these tears of self-
realization that I see too much in
what we are or can't be?

Oh, Life, when will we learn that
change is the metamorphosis of our
existence molded by the will of
time?

Oh, Life, I am yours. Whatever it is you want of me I am ready to give.

WILLIAM STEIG

Journey

Our thirst guides us to seek the water
of life and the oasis of our dreams
that fills our bowl.

The path toward life's meaning is a
mixture of happiness and strife that
no one can escape.

The truth shall be known to those
who open their conscious mind to the
vision of beauty that is hidden
within.

We are born into the grace of our
existence; time is given to carry out
life's sacred duty to fulfill our
purpose.

With every step, we grow into our
wisdom, and the journey through life
is a path we choose to create.

We are the guests in infinite time;
slow down your steps and savor this
moment before it escapes your
consciousness.

Your journey is in your own hands, and the choices
you will make over the course of your life
will shape your destiny in the future.

NOZER KANGA

All Within

Infinity within infinity, to the infinite
degree, is our destiny, drifting into
the vastness of time with every
moment of our existence.

Darkness within darkness is our
degree of darkness, where even light
can't touch the soul of our being.

Nothingness within nothingness is
our degree of emptiness, which is not
even the abyss of our imagination
that the mind can't reach.

Eternity within eternity to the eternal
degree is when we reflect upon our
existence with humility of our
insignificance.

Shades within shades are the degree
to which our shadowy world of
illusions unveils our vision of reality,
that we long to see.

Consciousness within consciousness
is our degree of conscious
awareness, in which the depth of our
mind is realized.

Life within death is our degree of
living in which joy and suffering
change within us like night and day.

> We cross infinity with every step; we
> meet eternity in every second.
>
> **RABINDRANATH TAGORE**

Time At Hand

The rich will spend their lives
hoarding wealth, which death will
come to collect at their time's end.

Time moves like an ageless river, a
momentary life in one second,
reflected on the water of our reality.

Infinite time lost in our dreams
travels through our consciousness in
a single night, only to be realized in
our moment of awakening.

Will we ever wake up and come out
of our hidden ways to seek the light
that time reflects in our eyes?

Why chase the wind that is bound
under the stillness of our breath, sit
still and enjoy the breeze.

Can we uphold our existence and
give up our blind pleasures to
overcome worldly death when that
time comes to collect?

Was it a dream or the reality of a
dream that escaped time and drifted
back into the universe?

To every one of us, there must come a time when the whole universe will be found to have been a dream, when we find the soul is infinitely better than its surroundings. It is only a question of time, and time is nothing in the infinite.

SAI BABA

In Time

There is one moment, and no other,
to bring our existence back into the
moment when we reflect on
ourselves for a moment.

We have walked forward and
backward, giving our spirit no time
for self-fulfillment in our journey
through life that runs in circles.

Our mind will take us deep into
reality to seek our conscious will
through moments of self-reflection.

The world's beauty is infused with
passion, which poetry distills in our
moments to give to the world.

Why do we burden life with things
that weigh too much with gravity if
liberating the spirit is what will
lighten our burden?

If we run too fast, time will move
quickly and become a conscious blur
in our gaze, altering our perception
of being.

At the end-point, there is nothing but being,
no time but the present.

RABBI AKIVA TATZ

Path I Take

I will walk into the light to overcome
the darkness of my human nature and
seek the path that will make me
whole.

I will walk into myself to shed the
burden of my earthly existence and
find the spirit that will lift me into
the spacious sky.

I will walk into the world to cleanse
away my humanity with holy water
that will fulfill the thirst of my human will.

I will walk into my mind to lift the
veil from my hidden consciousness
and see the beauty of my emerging
imagination.

I will walk into my spirit to embrace
the lonely soul that awaits me with
restless longing.

I will walk into Nature to immerse
myself in the mystical light that
glows to color the essence of my
existence.

March on. Do not tarry. To go forward is to move
toward perfection. March on, and fear not
the thorns or the sharp
stones on life's path.

KHALIL GIBRAN

Path I Seek

I have become the seeker of the
world that lays bare the beauty of
light into a vision my eyes long to
see.

The path I seek moves my mind to
give these searching eyes the vision
to complete life's journey.

I have become the seeker of my
wisdom that questions the nature of
what has made me human.

The path I seek opens like a veil,
uncovering the mystical reality that
flirts with my conscious eyes.

I have become the seeker of my
consciousness that looks deep into
the crevasses of my fractured mind.

The path I seek is beyond the
illusions of reality that pave the road
to my forgotten dreams.

I have become the seeker of wisdom,
the shadow of my being embraced by
the warmth of a candle's light.

Seek only light and freedom, and do not immerse yourself too deeply in the worldly mire.

VINCENT VAN GOGH

Dust in Dust

Wisdom only comes when faced
with a moral dilemma that rages in
our souls and burns us with doubt.

Your choice will determine your fate
as you embark on a steadfast mortal
journey to seek the truth within
yourself.

Courage breaks the will of doubt and
carries you through the uncertainty
of reality that comes at you with
worldly might.

Make a name for yourself by leaving
something good behind for posterity
to remember your spiritual deeds.

We will become an afterthought once
we become dust in the sweep of
time, and the wind will come to
collect and spread it back to the world.

The remnant of our existence is what
we have done, which becomes the
wisdom for humanity to spread into
tomorrow.

In the shadow of time, life takes the
first step into the darkened path that
will shed the light to our enlightened
vision.

Become dust, and they will throw thee in the air; Become stone, and they will throw thee on glass.

ALLAMA MUHAMMAD IQBAL

Let It Show

Will you teach me to love life and
humanity completely, never letting
them depart from the essence of my
heart?

Will you show me the way into your
soul when we seek each other on the
bridge between life and death?

Will you show me a glimpse of your
beauty, which my heart longs to see
in the mystical shades of your radiant
eyes?

Will you help me find myself when I
am lost chasing my conscious
dreams in the darkness of this world?

Will you walk with me to the end of
time, hand in hand, and never let me
lose what we have found in each
others' souls?

Will you enter the door of my
consciousness to bring my mind the
wisdom of your humble ways?

Will you shed the fragrance of your
love upon my spirit that is swelling
with emotions for your mystical
beauty?

A Sufi holy man was asked what forgiveness is. He said, "It is the fragrance that flowers give when they are crushed."

UNKNOWN SUFI

Make It Happen

All things are possible when the
mind shatters the uncertainty of our
doubts by being spontaneous in the
moral act of giving.

All things are possible when we walk
with wisdom, achieving a thousand-
mile journey with every step.

All things are possible when we open
our eyes to the light of our
imagination to seek the beauty of our
creative minds.

All things are possible when
humanity builds the future of
civilization by learning to preserve
what is old and crumbling in time.

All things are possible when we love
with the passion of our spirit and
welcome all that comes through our
doors.

All things are possible when we
realize the impossible and make it
possible by the strength of our
human character.

All things are possible when the
spirit of our existence soars into the
sky with wings of freedom that will
not touch the ground.

A frog decided to reach the top of a tree. All frogs shouted, "It's impossible, it's impossible . . ." Still, the frog reached the top . . . How? Because He was DEAF . . . And He thought everyone was encouraging. him to reach the top. "BE DEAF TO NEGATIVE THOUGHTS. IF YOUR AIM IS TO REACH YOUR GOAL"

BUDDHA

Silence, We Hear

In moments of silence, time holds us
still as eternity takes silent steps into
our conscious world.

In moments of silence, we reflect on
life's wisdom as we begin at the
beginning and move toward our end,
with poetic foresight in our silent
journey.

In moments of silence, our spiritual
voice calls us to lift the veil from our
eyes, allowing us to see the beauty of
our existence reflected in the mirror
of silent reflections.

In moments of silence, we shed tears
for the time wasted as we grow old,
running toward our end with our
gaze fixed on the fading
distance.

In moments of silence, we embrace
the ones we love and hold them close
before they leave our world with their
silent farewell.

In moments of silence, the world
slips from our consciousness, settling
in our dreams beneath the silent,
mystical night.

I never saw any land shining more brilliantly than the lamp of silence.

BAYAZID BASTAMI

Eternity of Time

In our eternal silence, the mind
moves through the vastness of
consciousness as our thoughts reflect
on the words we utter.

In our eternal vision, the eyes will
see beyond the boundaries of reality
as light guides us through the
darkness of our world.

In our eternal quest for meaning, we
seek ourselves only to realize how
lost we have become in our fast-
moving world.

We realize how short and narrow our
experience can be when we run blind
with eyes that will not open to the
vision of eternal time.

In our eternal need to find happiness,
we sow the seeds of joy that will
grow roots in our souls.

In our eternal mind, we come to
write our story with the conscious
will of our moving pen.

In our eternal love for human
dignity, we bow in humility to the
wisdom of our humble nature.

Silence is as deep as eternity, speech
as shallow as time.

THOMAS CARLYLE

The Great Task

We work toward the good of
humanity the moment we become
aware of our mortal existence.

We work toward the perfection of
our human nature the moment we
live a life that reflects our humility.

We strive to create beauty for the
world to behold, the moment we
radiate the light of truth from our
burning souls.

We strive to find happiness by
bringing our conscious dreams to life
in joyful ways.

We work toward the act of our deeds
the moment we give ourselves to the
betterment of others.

We work toward a path that maps out
our journey, the moment we move
with momentum in our human spirit.

We strive to uncover the truth that
opens our minds to a world that will
embrace our spiritual wisdom.

> The offering of wisdom is better than any material offering, Arjuna, for the goal of all work is spiritual wisdom.
>
> **BHAGAVAD GITA**

Fading Steps

Take the courage to move ahead in
your destined path. Carry your spirit
with love for yourself, and you will
achieve all you want in life.

Your strength will empower your
mind, which will lead you into the
eternity of your purpose with your
fading footsteps.

But we can never be blind to the
truth when our eyes are open to the
vision of our moral ways.

You are lost and will never be found
once you lose your direction in your
destined path toward life's journey.

Keep faith in your heart and give it
to your soul; that is the only way to
find harmony in the sanctity of your
existence in time.

Our footsteps are freed to run into
the realm of time, giving life the
space to find itself.

The journey of a lifetime is the
adventure the mind seeks with its
wandering thoughts that drift into its
imagination.

Do not seek to follow in the footsteps of the wise. Seek what they sought.

MATSUO BASHO

Silent Time

Time holds us still in our silent
moments as eternity enters our
conscious minds, drawing on our
past to lay the path for our future.

In our silent moments, we reflect on
our life's journey from beginning to
end, with wisdom and foresight, as
we move through time.

In our silent moments, we listen to
our spirit, which voices our essence
to humanity and binds us with the
wisdom of worldly experience.

In our silent moments, we often
regret the time we wasted when we
grow old, coming face to face with
our end.

In our silent moments, we extend our
hand to the ones we love and
embrace them before they leave our
world.

In our silent moments, we meditate
on the meaning of life, which
embodies the wisdom of our inner
thoughts.

In our moments of silence, dreams
gather into the night, shedding our
consciousness into the rivers of
reality.

Silence is an ocean. Speech is a river. When the ocean is searching for you. Don't walk into the river. Listen to the ocean.

RUMI

Captive Will

Trapped in our conscious existence,
we can no longer bargain with the
lost time that leaves our hands
too quickly.

Trapped in our intellectual minds, we
can no longer think beyond the
reasoning capacity of our
imagination.

Trapped in worldly pleasures, we are
left impoverished when we neglect
our human spirit and chase
far reaching dreams.

Trapped in our need for self-
realization, we hold the light that
reflects on the mirror of our inner
reality.

Trapped in our moral dilemma, we
are lured into the delusions of truth
that take us away from our conscious
Self.

Trapped in our rigid ways, we are
shattered when we collide with the
harsh reality of our broken fate.

Trapped in our moment of creation,
we grow into the world with
conscious wonder rooted in the
beauty of our existence.

Here we are, trapped in the amber of the moment. There is no why.

KURT VONNEGUT

No Fear

Do not fear the moment of battle; we
must fight for what is morally right
and remain steadfast against the
banality of evil.

Do not fear the moment of
uncertainty; hope will burn with
revelation when you open your soul
with the strength of your faith.

Do not fear life's sufferings, for those
carrying the weight of their existence
will free their mind from the
hardship of reality.

Do not fear the power of others, for
they will become feeble the moment
they try to flaunt their hold over
humanity.

Do not fear the long journey through
time, for once taken, the meaning of
life begins to unravel under the
landscape of your reality.

Do not fear the grandness of
ideas, for once envisioned, they will
transform your mind and inspire the
world.

Do not fear the knowledge that you
seek, for the intelligence you come
to know will humble your mind.

Where the mind is without fear and the head is held high is where knowledge is free.

RABINDRANATH TAGORE

What Will Come?

The future will hold no meaning till
we reflect on what we want to be
today by reflecting on what we lost
yesterday.

The future will never come to us
unless we move toward it, leaving a
trail of footsteps behind.

The future will never be realized
until we seize this moment, which
will reflect who we will be
tomorrow.

The future will never come to us if
we are anchored to our past and
unable to come to terms with who
we are today.

The future will never come to us if
we continue to chase the wind and
never sit still to enjoy the breeze.

The future will never come to us if
the conscious Self can't grasp the
vastness of time that comes to embrace
us.

The future is distant, and the past is
near, but this moment is the closest
when we do not let it escape our
consciousness.

The past is already gone; the future is not yet here.
There's only one moment for you to live,
and that is the present moment

BUDDHA

Caught In Eternity

Eternity races through our mind's
eyes as we walk through time with a
blurring glimpse of our fading
existence.

Eternity gets caught in our moment
of self-realization as we remain
hidden under the veil of our
conscious reflection.

Eternity comes through nothingness,
and nothing comes through eternity
except the will of eternity to the
eternal degree.

Eternity moves through the vastness
of our universe, yet it is only realized
when we are at the end of our reach.

Eternity is the spirit of infinite love;
the greater the joy of love, the
greater the eternal bliss in our life.

Eternity is the light of our distant
past that races through our
consciousness with conscious speed
to awaken our perception of reality.

Time is but the stream I go a-fishing in. I drink at it; but while I drink, I see the sandy bottom and detect how shallow it is. Its thin current slides away, but eternity remains.

HENRY DAVID THOREAU

Breathe

With every breath, we breathe in the
conscious awareness of ourselves
and breathe out the air of our mortal
existence.

With every breath, we are awakened
by the need to feel the eternity of
time and exhale the forgotten
moments of our past.

With every breath, the words of our
minds are etched into our
consciousness as we breathe out the
streams of thoughts written by our
flowing imagination.

With every breath, the silent air
moves in and out of our lips as we
breathe out the scent of our
conscious emotions.

With every breath, the eyes remain
serene as they gaze beyond the
horizon, taking in the infinite vision
of our ever-changing landscape.

With every breath, we hold ourselves
to the world in our human ways,
breathing out the raw nature of our
primordial Self.

When you arise in the morning, think of what a precious privilege it is to be alive - to breathe, to think, to enjoy, to love.

MARCUS AURELIUS

Calm Stillness

Be still in your reflection; time will
carry you on your journey with silent
steps, moving through life with ease.

Be still in your mind's imagination,
and your thoughts will mold you into
the spirit of being human.

Be still in your vision of reality; you
will see the nuances of life's deep
mystical secrets reflected in your
consciousness.

Be still in the calm of your emotional
storm, and the rays of sunshine will
dawn upon you with radiance of
hope.

Be still in the fire that burns in your
heart; the warmth of love will
comfort you in life from this cold
world of humanity.

The stillness of your conscious
moments and the uncertainty of life
will settle into your mind like dust in
time.

Be still in the light of your conscious
vision, and the darkness of reality
will merge into the colors of life.

Once I knew only darkness and stillness . . . my life was without a past or future... but a little word from the fingers of another fell into my hand that clutched at emptiness, and my heart leaped to the rapture of living.

HELEN KELLER

Bending Time

The miracle of birth liberates our
spirit from time, giving us the mind
of consciousness to seek our
existence.

The origin of light gave us the vision
to see through the darkness of
reality, bringing us out into the world
to gaze at the beauty of creation.

The fire of our imagination gave us
the curiosity to burn away the
vestiges of our primitive nature.

The wisdom of humanity has given
us the spirit to reason our way out of
the chaos of reality, which is in flux
with time.

The will of our human nature pushed
us to seek the universe by bending
the infinity of time with the gravity
of our intelligence.

The power of perception gave us the
humility to accept the limits of what
we can understand with our drifting
minds.

The man never feels the want of what it
never occurs to him to ask for.

ARTHUR SCHOPENHAUER

Being Born

The birth of our spirit helps us grow
into the world, and the moment we
realize our existence, we are reborn
again in time, so eternal.

The birth of our consciousness
awakens us to the light of eternity,
reawakening the moment our eyes
absorb the colors imbued with the
beauty of life.

The birth of humanity moves us to
seek humility, and the moment we
find virtue, we shed our pride for the
conscious world.

The birth of love blossoms in our
souls, and the moment we are
awakened, we let it enter our hearts
to thaw our coldest emotions.

The birth of knowledge awakens our
minds, and we are reborn when
conscious wonder takes hold of our
runaway thoughts.

The birth of eternity is lost in time,
and we become prisoners in its reach
the moment we are born.

We should weep for men at their birth,
not at their death.

MONTESQUIEU

Time's Bargain

Oh, time, you are my beginning and
end, and yet you gave me a glimpse
of direction to take my first step into
life's journey.

Oh, time, you flow like a seamless
river ever expanding into the
landscape, and yet you gave me a
glimpse of joy to seek my reflection
in your mystical water.

Oh, time, you give us the wisdom to
write our unwritten story, yet our
conscious mind can't find the words
to express our eternal truth.

Oh, time; how can we bargain with
your ever-giving spirit when we
waste so much and keep asking for
more?

Oh, time, the warmth of your light
awakens our souls as we try to live in
your humble domain with sincerity
of heart.

Oh, time, youth runs through your
fields with no worries for tomorrow,
yet we age too quickly, reflecting on
what we were with broken sorrow.

Hide nothing, for time, which sees all and hears all, exposes all.

SOPHOCLES

Path I Lay

I am the way into myself; the
moment I turn outward is when I
reflect inward in search of my soul.

I am the way into your life's journey;
the moment the path is laid before
my feet, I take my first step into the
vastness of this world.

I am the way into my words; the
moment my mind recognizes that the
perception of reality is thoughts
formed in my consciousness.

I am the way of this world; the
moment I come to terms with my
humanity, humility takes refuge in
my wisdom.

I am the way into the vision of light;
the moment darkness casts its
shadow upon my spirit is when I am
born into the world.

I am the way into the beauty of
Nature; the moment my heart
awakens is when love walks through
my doors with unhindered emotions.

I am the Way, the Truth, and the Life. No one comes to the Father except through me.

JESUS CHRIST

Life's Road

We journey through life with many
winding roads, searching for the path
to salvation, only to find it twisting
and changing before our eyes.

We journey through our mystical
dreams deep into the night, only to
be awakened by the whispering
sound of the sighing breeze.

We journey through our minds to
seek our conscious reality, only to
find that our conscious perception
liberates us from the tangled
thoughts that bind us.

We journey through infinite time,
searching for our beginnings and
ends, only to be entangled within the
ever-changing mold of our reality.

We journey through the heart of
creation to seek the vision of love,
only to be shattered into fragments
by life's hard lessons.

We journey through our minds,
searching for insight into our human
thoughts, only to lose ourselves in
the absolutes of reason and logic.

It's your road and yours alone. Others may walk it with you, but no one can walk it for you.

RUMI

Hidden Wisdom

A moment of reflection holds time
still as we gaze into the conscious
mirrors of our existence, fully
reflected in ourselves.

A moment of contemplation in our
minds holds us in silent thoughts as
we gaze into our imagination, fully
transformed by our words.

A moment of stillness holds our feet
firm to the ground as we gaze into
the path of our journey with humility
in our will.

A moment of consciousness enters
our soul as we gaze within ourselves
for meaning, for the hidden wisdom
to unveil itself.

A moment of acceptance is all that
we need to humble ourselves as we
gaze into the blemishes of our human
imperfections with complete
acceptance.

A moment of escape from reality
lures us into our dreams as we sleep
away time, liberating us from our
imprisoned world.

By three methods we may learn wisdom: First,
by reflection, which is noblest; Second,
by imitation, which is easiest; and
third by experience,
which is the bitterest.

CONFUCIUS

Rejoice In Life

Let us celebrate the time we hold in
our hands, for there is no greater
tomorrow than the moment we have
been given today.

Let us celebrate the health of our
being, for there is no greater gift than
the peace we hold sacred in our
hearts.

Let us celebrate the people we love,
for there is no greater pleasure than
to be embraced by the ones we love.

Let us celebrate the time that fills us
with joy, for there is no greater
happiness than to run free into the
world with laughter on our faces.

Let us celebrate children at play, for
there is no greater wisdom in life
than to become a child once more.

Let us celebrate the beauty of
creation that gave us life, for there is
no greater miracle than being alive in
the beauty of our world.

All my life through, the new sights of Nature made me rejoice like a child.

MARIE CURIE

Bring It Out

Let all you do become the mosaic of
your vision in the fragments of
broken time that our world will strive
to see.

Let all that you say become the truth
that washes away the darkness from
the world that we come to see.

Let all you give become the act of
humility in the compassion of this
world we hope to see.

Let all be in your vision of humanity
become a conscious fire for the
world we all want to see.

Let all that you build in your creative
imagination transform the landscape
of the world that we all seek to see.

Let all that your poetic vision of this
world becomes what we all aspire to
see.

Let all you live for paint the reality
that reflects onto the world with
luminous light in colors that our
conscious mind wills to see.

When we seek to discover the best in others, we somehow bring out the best in ourselves.

WILLIAM ARTHUR WARD

Binding Love

Let us walk out into the vastness of
eternity and come back holding
nothing but the will to love.

Let us open our doors to the one who
comes into our hearts to become the
guest for life in the oneness of love.

Let us bind the truth to our human
spirit and untangle the knots of time,
so we can walk free into the world
and find true love.

Let us tap into our mind's wisdom,
which will pave the way to finding
the salvation we seek in the vision of
love.

Let us trace the time that moves us
forward, leaving behind the etched
memories of our lingering past that
we still love.

Let us voice the music of our
happiness and dance in the circle of
life, singing the joy of laughter that
fills us with love.

Let us meet on the bridge of life,
where the soul can embrace the spirit
it loves.

You do not do evil to those who do evil to you, but you deal with them with forgiveness and kindness.

PROPHET MUHAMMAD (PBUH)

Final Act

And above all, the true path to
yourself begins with the act of self-
giving and self-sacrifice.

And above all, those who dare to
move beyond their boundaries are
the ones who will achieve a
meaningful existence.

And above all, the world will never
achieve peace and harmony until the
collective consciousness of humanity
holds sacred the absolute sanctity of
life.

Above all, let the truth be your
guide, and the willfulness of your
mind will lead you toward the path
of Self-understanding.

Above all, let your creative
imagination take you on a journey
toward knowledge and give you the
intelligence to share it with
humanity.

Above all, let the world know that
your life has meaning, and you shall
fulfill your purpose written by your
willful spirit.

Above the cloud with its shadow is the star with its light.
Above all things, reverence thyself.

PYTHAGORAS

Searching

I shall seek you on the bridge of
time, where age will finally meet
your fading youth in each other's
eyes.

I shall seek you with my lonely steps
upon this winding road where the
journey through life will hold my
beginning toward your end.

I shall seek you in the cave of my
soul, where the beauty of your light
will comfort my eyes from the
darkness of this world.

I shall seek you in the landscape of
reality where the earth meets the sky,
under the falling horizon of my
spiritual gaze.

I shall seek you on the river of my
dreams, where two wandering souls
become one under the shades of the
moonlit night.

I shall seek you amid time as you
become the dewdrops that cling to
the lips of my thirsty soul.

So, I say to you, keep on asking, and it will
be given to you; keep on seeking,
and you will find, keep
on knocking, and it will
be opened to you.

LUKE 11:9

Time of Being

The breath of our existence is to take
in the world with our conscious soul
and come out fully molded by the
hands of time.

The vision of our existence is to see
the world in our conscious reflection
and emerge fully reflected in the
mirrors of time.

The will of our existence is to walk
in this world with conscious steps
and come out fully humanized in the
wisdom of time.

The mind of our existence is to see
the world fully understood and come
into our consciousness, nurtured by
time.

The spirit of our existence is to touch
the world with our embracing hearts
and come out fully loved by the
giving of time.

The soul of our existence is to seek
ourselves and come out fully
revealed in the emergence of time.

The beauty of our existence is to fall
in love with Nature and come out in
our garden of reality, enriched by the
fragrance of time.

Dwell in peace in the home of your own being,
and the messenger of death will
not be able to touch you.

GURU NANAK

I Am Yours

I will be your guest for eternity when
you welcome me at your door and
take me into your home with
compassion in your heart.

I will be your true lover who will
make you whole when you hold me
in your heart and take me in with
your loving gaze.

I will be the beauty in your soulful
eyes when you open them, my way,
and take me in with the sincerity of
love with your smile.

I will be the voice that awakens you
from your dreams as dawn whispers
to you to take me in as your
conscious reality.

I will be the air that gives you life, as
the breath of wisdom asks you to
take me in with your meditative
mind.

I will be the eternity in your
momentary existence, as time asks
your mortality to take me in as your
humble friend.

I will be what you are to yourself
when you take me in as a river
moving toward your ocean.

If I am not for myself, who will be for me?
If I am not for others, what am I?
And if not now, when?

RABBI HILLEL

What You Do

And whatever you want to do in life,
take a moment to reflect and savor
the time that awakens you from your
conscious dreams.

And whatever you hold in your
heart, take a moment to love and
savor the joy that elevates your
emotions with the sound of laughter.

And whatever you fear in the
uncertainty of life, take a moment to
find hope and savor the courage that
moves your spirit to seek the truth.

And whatever you see in the
darkness of your mind, take a
moment to reflect on your thoughts
and savor the vision that will move
you toward the wisdom of light.

And whatever you create in your
world of inspiration, take a moment
to observe and savor what is revealed
to your imagination.

And whatever you bring to humanity,
take a moment to share and savor the
humility of all that you give to this
empty world.

Lose not yourself in a far-off time, seize
the moment that is thine.

FRIEDRICH SCHILLER

If You Knew

If I ask you to transcend the
boundaries of time, will you pursue
the infinite vision in your conscious
journey to transform the world?

If I tell you to let light unveil your
darkness, will you see the infinite
shades of wisdom that will enter your
consciousness?

If I tell you to voice the thoughts that
brew in your mind, will you hear the
infinite sounds of meaning in your
poetic words?

If I tell you to walk out into the
world with your mystical gaze, will
you see the beauty of infinite love
that lives in your heart?

If I tell you to feel the movement of
the gentle breeze, will you sense the
breath of passion that leaves your
soul breathless?

If I tell you to awaken the majestic
nature of your conscious spirit, will
you not know the beauty of life that
distills in your eyes?

Yesterday I was clever, so I wanted to change the world. Today I am wise, so I am changing myself.

RUMI

Virtuous Way

The virtue of living in your simple
ways gives you the time to savor
your life with the freedom to seek
the fruits of success in this world.

The virtue of walking in your
humble ways gives you the wisdom
to move out into the world with no
burden from time under your feet.

The virtue of kindness in your deeds
gives you the joy of wonder that will
foresee the purpose of your life's
journey.

The virtue of seeking knowledge will
give you the intelligence to know the
wisdom in your moral judgments in
human reasoning.

The virtue of love will give your
heart the empathy to feel the human
emotions that emanate from a world
of suffering.

The virtue of surrendering your will
to humanity is letting go of your
pride, which pulls you into the abyss
of darkness before your eyes.

To practice five things under all circumstances constitutes perfect virtue; these five are gravity, generosity of soul, sincerity, earnestness, and kindness.

CONFUCIUS

Forgotten Time

Memories linger in our mind's eye,
racing through the corridors of our
timeless dreams with fading
footsteps.

Memories etched in time fall into our
conscious mind, leaving subtle
impressions of the life stories of our
forgotten past.

Memories caught in the waves of our
emotions wash ashore into our hearts,
leaving a lasting impression that still
lingers today.

Memories steeped in the love of life
become the written moments in our
silent tears, which wash away the
feelings we once had for each other.

Memories lie in the dust of time,
leaving the footprint of our past as
we drift further into the world we
seek tomorrow.

Memories ferment in conscious time,
aged wisdom ripened by the beauty
of our youthful ways that once held
us with vitality.

Memories lift from our conscious
eye like smoke rising from the
embers of our burning past.

Memory and forgetfulness are as life and death
to one another. To live is to remember, and
to remember is to live. To die is
to forget, and to forget is to die.

SAMUEL BUTLER

The Blessed Life

The blessing of time becomes our
mind's journey, allowing us to
wander freely into the enormity of
our worldly imagination.

The blessing of conscious reflection
gives us the awareness to seek
wisdom and run freely into the deep
valleys of our human existence.

The blessing of life's birth is the
miracle of our beginning, which
becomes the water in the clay of our
spiritual mold, shaped by the will of
time.

The blessing of light reflects in our
eyes, giving us the vision to see the
infinite colors of Nature's beauty.

The blessings of love will make us
whole and give us the grace to face
the evil of our human nature.

The blessing of our faith will give us
the strength to bear the many storms
of life's journey that will come our
way.

Blessing others is to be blessed when
the sincerity of giving becomes a
beautiful act of humility.

Blessed is he who expects nothing, for he shall never be disappointed.

JONATHAN SWIFT

Story of Time

Time will give us the fruit of our
work, but we let it go to waste when
we chase the sweetness of our
unfulfilled dreams.

Time will escape through our mind's
eye when we sleep, leaving our
conscious moments behind, never
realizing that reality has already left
our senses.

Time will never come back to us
when we are anchored to our past
and fearful of what tomorrow will
bring.

Time will determine our every step,
but what will determine our fate is
what we seek and where we look.

Time will line our faces with the
weathering of age, and we will look
in the mirror to trace life's
moments reflected in our eyes.

Time will write the story in the pages
of our existence, line by line, word
by word, to reflect with written
experience etched upon our
conscious mind.

Time will come to us like a shadow
lost in the light, giving us the vision
to find ourselves in the mold of our
changing existence.

Time and memory are true artists; they remold reality nearer to the heart's desire.

JOHN DEWEY

Fulfillment

The sweetness of life is never bitter
when you taste it with the love of
your giving spirit by sharing it with
the world.

The thirst for life will drown our
souls when we drink our fate with
our own two hands.

The warmth of our smile will never
tarnish our hearts when laughter
casts a glow on humanity like
heavenly rays of sunshine.

The fragrance of life will awaken our
senses when we take time to breathe
in the mystical essence of our
spiritual nature.

The world's beauty will soothe our
emotions when we open our minds to
reflect it in our conscious eyes.

The splendor of life will keep us
young as time holds all meaning in
the eternity of unbound love.

The river seeks the ocean, just as
light seeks darkness, and when the
two meet, their true nature is revealed.

The desires of this world are like seawater.
The more you drink of them, the
more you thirst.

IBN ARABI

Within

There is infinite within Infinity to the
never-ending degree, but that is
limitless to the one who seeks it
endlessly.

Nothing is within nothingness, yet all
things come through it, but they
become nothing the moment we
pursue them as being real.

There is truth within truth layered in
the wisdom of time, but it will not
become true until we live it with our
whole being.

There are shadows within shadows,
layered in darkness from which all
light comes through as the vision we
become to see when we open our eyes.

There is a consciousness within
consciousness that pierces through
our willful mind, awakening the Self
to conscious awareness.

There is an end to our beginning and
a beginning to our end, but that will
never come into being until we bring
ourselves into the moment of our being.

There is time before and time after
our existence, but the immortal soul
will remain beyond time in its
spiritual nature.

We cannot teach people anything; we can only help them discover it within themselves.

GALILEO GALILEI

Dreams Within

We take refuge in the hope that one
day, time will ease our burden of life
so that we can live in the harmonious
joy of our happiness.

We take refuge in our hearts so that,
one day, love can enter our spirits
and become our guests for eternity.

We take refuge in our minds so that
one day, we can reason with
ourselves to live in the beauty of
mystical awareness.

We take refuge in our conscious
reality so that one day, we can feel
the colors of emotions stirred by the
nature of light.

We can take refuge in our deep
sadness so that one day, joy can
come and carry it all away.

We can take refuge in our moments
of silence so that one day we can
voice the music of love that enters
our hearts.

My dreams were all my own; I accounted for them to
nobody; they were my refuge when annoyed.
My dearest pleasure when free.

MARY SHELLEY

The Giving

I want the stillness in my silent
moments to hear the words that are
music to my ears and wisdom to my
soul.

I want the fruit of my life's work, so
I can offer it to the world for them to
savor it with the purity of its
wisdom.

I want the burden of living so I can
carry it against the gravity of my
mind and hold it up to the world to
see how it's lifted.

I want the charm of love to seep into
the crevices of my emotions and
drown my will in the aftertaste of
eternal longing.

I want the beauty that falls upon my
eyes so that I can take it into my
soul with my loving gaze.

I want the life no one wants to live,
so I can become conscious of my
will, which will build my character
from the ground up.

I want the wisdom to humble my
pride so I can shed my human nature
before I leave this world.

Generosity is giving more than you can, and pride is taking less than you need.

KHALIL GIBRAN

Act of Being

We are committed to the air we
breathe into our being; without it, we
can never sustain our humble
existence.

We are committed to the will to live
in our spiritual domain, without
which our souls can never complete
their human journey.

We are committed to the love we
hold in our hearts, without which we
can never blossom in the beauty of
our growing compassion.

We are committed to finding our
purpose in life, without which the
path to wisdom can never be
realized.

We are committed to the human
spirit that seeks the simple virtues of
this world, without which we can
never find meaning in our humble
morality.

We are committed to a life that lives
in the streams of time, without which
there is no reason for us to come into
this world.

He who has no attachments can love others,
for his love is pure and divine. And it is
from those small acts of love
that you truly can be happy.

BHAGAVAD GITA

Art of Wisdom

The art of giving becomes your spirit
of receiving when you house the
suffering of humanity with your
heart of kindness.

The art of humility is giving yourself
to others, and you will receive
human compassion with your ever-
loving grace.

The art of living is to walk with time,
and the adventure of the world will
become your life's journey.

The art of wisdom is to strive for the
truth and listen to your conscience,
which whispers the virtue of
morality in your ways of living.

The art of will speaks to your
actions, and the deeds of your
humanity bring compassion into
being.

The art of love is total surrender, and
the passion of loving consumes the
soul in the oneness of love.

The art of reflection is to see
yourself as you are, and the mirror
will reflect what the truth shall
reveal.

The aim of art is to represent not the outward appearance of things, but their inward significance.

ARISTOTLE

Humility

We are at the mercy of time that
keeps us moving, even when life
holds us still in the silence of our
changing thoughts.

We are at the mercy of our will,
which moves us further into a world
that goes against the wisdom of our
inner voice.

We are at the mercy of our human
pride, which will not allow us to live
a life of simplicity.

We are at the mercy of our desires,
which keeps us attached to the
pleasures we continue pursuing till
our very end.

We are at the mercy of moving
experiences that keep us chasing
knowledge that keeps escaping our
understanding.

We are at the mercy of uncertainty
that engulfs us in darkness, yet it
strengthens our faith, as we wait for
the coming of the light of revelation.

We are at the mercy of our human
nature, which seeks insatiable desires
that can never be fulfilled in our
lifetime.

Teach me to feel another's woe, to hide the fault I
see that mercy I to others show,
that mercy shows to me.

ALEXANDER POPE

Those Who

But those who reflect on their lives
will see the light reflected in their
spirit, revealing the path their mind
must take through conscious
reflection.

But those who choose the longer
path toward their journey will often
find the shortest way to fulfilling the
quest for a meaningful existence.

But those who pursue the simplest
pleasures in life will have time to
savor every joy they are given.

But those who breathe slowly and
deeply will feel the breath of
calmness that brings mystical
serenity into their spirit.

But those who seek the good in their
hearts will find the love of the world
that will come to embrace their souls
in due time.

But those who seek beauty within
themselves will find the reflection of
the love that makes all things
beautiful when realized.

But those who seek the wisdom to
become human will find the soul of
virtue growing in their humanity
with every act.

Good things come to those who wait, but great things come to those who endure.

MATSHONA DHLIWAYO

Not Anyone

Let no one declare that your life is
not worth its weight in gold except
time, which will measure it by how
much you weigh it against yourself.

Let no one convince you that you
can't accomplish what your mind
pursues and do the impossible when
passion brings it into being.

Let no one tell you that your life's
dreams are not worth pursuing, and
the vision to bring them into reality
is not worth the time.

Let no one steal the beauty of love
that lurks in your heart and makes
you feel the emptiness of your
dwindling emotions.

Let no one take away the hope to
wash away the sorrow that lingers in
your life and steal your faith that will
uplift your spirit.

Let no one erase your purpose in life
and propel you toward the blind
vision of this world that will be your
end.

Spread love everywhere you go. Let no one ever come to you without leaving you happier.

MOTHER TERESA

Spirit of Hope

There is hope for the human spirit
when it looks out into the world with
wonder and reflection in its eyes.

There is hope for humanity when it
unites its collective spirit to uphold
the moral character of civilization.

There is hope for the lost world
when it finds the conscious vision to
seek its purpose with its willful
mind.

There is hope in the sanctity of love
when virtue conceals our beauty to
guard it from the envious eyes of the
world.

There is hope for our blindness when
we open our eyes into the darkness
to see the vision of light revealing
our humanity.

There is hope for a life that is lived
with time and not wasted when given
with gracious offerings to our human
spirit.

The real meaning of enlightenment is to gaze with undimmed eyes on all darkness.

NIKOS KAZANTZAKIS

Willful Time

Time will move us in all directions,
yet the stillness of our mind holds
time still in our conscious thoughts.

Time will age us in many ways, yet
the wisdom we gain will make time
eternal for our human spirit.

Time will escape us when the world
absorbs us, yet conscious reflection
will bring time back when we see it
with our imagined mind.

Time breaks the mold of our
existence, yet the human spirit will
guard us against it as we walk out
into the world, uncertain of our
direction.

Time is like a river that moves
silently in its willful purpose, yet
only finds salvation when it becomes
one with our living ocean.

Time will seek us in our conscious
journey, yet it will give us the
freedom of day and night to find
ourselves.

Life has no meaning the moment you lose
the illusion of being eternal.

JEAN-PAUL SARTRE

The Tragic Fate

The greatest tragedy in life occurs when
you devalue yourself for the value of
others who come to value you even
less.

The great tragedy in life occurs when you
waste time chasing the wind, which
leaves you breathless for air you
can't breathe.

The great tragedy in life occurs when you
become irrelevant to the world that
only sees you as dust in the passing
wind.

The great tragedy in life occurs when losing
your purpose and wandering, seeking
meaning while stumbling through the
world blind.

The great tragedy in life occurs when you
don't see the beauty of your spirit,
even when it is staring at you in the
mirror of self-reflection.

The great tragedy in life occurs when living in
your dreams and never waking up to
the truth that defines your reality in
the world.

The great tragedy in life occurs when you
imprison your mind in thoughts that
can't escape from the tangled
illusions you create.

The tragedy of life is what dies inside
a man while he lives.

ALBERT SCHWEITZER

Chapter 5: Mind, Body, Spirit, Soul, and Self

The soul of wisdom is etched in our
conscious mind, and the body will
embrace the Self that lives within.
The purpose of our existence is to
find the human spirit that will make
us whole. Over time, we become lost
in wonder as we ponder who, what,
and why we are here.

The body will thirst for life, but the
mind will hunger for self-realization.
What is the soul? Where does the
human spirit reside? What were we
before birth, and what will we be
after we die? What will become of
time when it finally ends? Our hearts
will question, and our minds will
seek to answer.

The many shades of meaning are
reflected in our eyes and
voiced to our spirit so we can see
them in the light of their existence.
Our imagination transcends the
boundaries of reality, the vision
to see beyond deepens our need for
relevancies in our journey in life.

The mind will seek what it does not
know, and our words will remain
elusive about what it knows. Only
when we humble ourselves does
intelligence seep into our thoughts,
and wisdom grows into our
perception. The measure of how
much we know is to realize how
little our minds can grasp.

"Many Shades of Wisdom"
represents the unity of our mind,
body, and spirit as we strive to seek
unity with the Self.

Will you awaken your mind to the perception of being by seeking the truth that merges with your consciousness?

SHAKOOR

Spirit of Wonder

The spirit of love is the dewdrops of
our human emotions that cling to our
hearts and blanket us with the
mystical warmth of Dawn's light.

The spirit of joy is the childhood
laughter that echoes in our souls and
comforts us from the coldness of our
worldly domain.

The spirit of purpose is to live in
every moment life gives us and make
every impression eternal in our silent
reflection.

The spirit of wisdom is to search for
meaning in the flux of time and
break free from the turbulence of our
human nature.

The spirit of our journey, ingrained
over time, propels us toward self-
fulfillment, driven by the vision of
discovery and wonder in our eyes.

The spirit of contentment is to go
beyond ourselves by letting go of
what we desire most, by giving it
back to the world.

Once we believe in ourselves, we can risk curiosity, wonder, spontaneous delight, or any experience that reveals the human spirit.

E. E. CUMMINGS

I Being Human

Oh, the spirit of my being: I am
blessed for all that you have given
me. You have opened my heart to
your light, which enters my soul and
erases all darkness from our eyes.

Oh, the spirit of my being: I am a
wandering mystic, searching for the
path that leads to your doors, as I
walk with the soles of my feet
toward my journey in this never-
ending time.

Oh, the spirit of my being: let me
open my eyes to the wisdom of your
reality to see the beauty of your light
that veils me from your truth.

Oh, the spirit of my being: let me
feel the colors of your creation and
smell the fragrance of life in the
fields of your roses.

Oh, the spirit of my being: let me
feel my inner emotions to awaken
my consciousness for the love of
your eternal grace.

Oh, the spirit of my being: let me
gather the fragments of my
existence, for you are the mosaic of
my universe that binds me to
yourself and makes me whole.

Challenging the meaning of life is the truest expression of the state of being human.

VIKTOR E. FRANKL

Eyes That Envision

The eyes of reality are upon our
spirit, and what we see reflects what
we want it to become.

The eyes of Nature have blossomed
in Spring's first bloom, and what
we'll grow is the love that Nature
brings into our hearts.

The eyes of pride have become the
veil of envy that will not free us from
darkness, nor let us see the light.

The eyes of love see deep into our
hearts, and what comes out are
waves of emotion that bow at our
feet in quiet surrender.

The eyes of laughter bring joy into
the world, and what rises is the mist
of hope that settles like dewdrops
upon our conscious reality.

The eyes of humanity seek our
human virtues, but the envious heart
of our jealous nature will hide them
from ever being seen by the world.

You left, and I cried tears of blood. My sorrow grows.
It's not just that You left. But when You left
my eyes went with You.
Now, how will I cry?

RUMI

Morality

In our righteous convictions, we
become the beacon of light for the
blind souls who do not see their
wayward path reflected in
their eyes.

In our righteous mind, reason
becomes our logical way of
navigating through our never-ending
maze of uncertainty in our ever-
changing thoughts.

In our righteous human spirit, we
take our first step into the world to
be transformed by experience and
shaped by the wisdom of time.

In our righteous moments of inner
reflection, we seek the truth that rises
from our conscious mind and lifts the
veil from the illusions of reality.

In our righteous act of Love, we
extend our hand to those who live in
darkness and bring them into the
light to see life's hidden beauty.

In our righteous deeds toward others,
we strive for moral good that paves
the road for humanity to walk toward
the grace of their human dignity.

The foolish are like ripples on water, for whatsoever they do is quickly effaced, but the righteous are like carvings upon stone, for their smallest act is durable.

HORACE

I Felt It

I feel you with my mind as my
words liberate from their meaning
and settle on the palms of your
conscious being.

I feel you in my dreams as time
melts away all realities that pull you
into my conscious soul.

I feel you with my heart when you
open the doors to your loving soul
with your conscious touch.

I feel you in the summer breeze as
the fragrance of life flirts and imbues
your spirit with my conscious
emotions.

I feel you in every heartbeat as the
rhythm of my existence becomes the
symphony of joy in your conscious
world.

I feel you in every breath I take,
which I take in with conscious
reverence.

I feel you in every wound that life
inflicts upon your soul. To heal, I
will nurture your spirit with my
conscious love.

Only those who have felt the knife can
understand the wound, only the
jeweler knows the nature
of the jewel.

MEERA

I Heard It

It was told to your mind: know
thyself through experience, and time
will wipe away the dust of your
ignorance.

It was told to your heart to love
yourself first, and then you can reach
out to the world to seek its loving
embrace.

It was told to the world that the
collective consciousness is our thirst
for salvation that binds us to the
humility we bring to our humanity.

It was told to the wisdom of age: let
the reflection of truth reveals us to
life, which shall hold us still under
the silence of our reflective eyes.

It was said that the freedom of our
will could never be liberated from
the human spirit, for the body holds
us too firmly to the ground.

It was said that the light of our vision
paints the colors of reality that are
never realized until we absorb them
into our conscious mind.

The highest and most beautiful things in life are not to be heard about, nor read about, nor seen, but, if one will, are to be lived.

SØREN KIERKEGAARD

It Comes

With the glory of time given, we
blossom with age as we augment our
human spirit with the wisdom of life.

Through the silence of self-
reflection, we learn to see the vision
of our true selves in the mirrors of
reality.

With the flesh of our bodily form, we
feel the emotions of love that cling
close to our lonely hearts.

With the courage of our will, we take
our first step into the long journey on
our faithful path toward life.

With the music of our soul, we sing
to the world the laughter of our
conscious awakening.

In the poetry of Nature's beauty, we
color our imagination with mystical
thoughts that only the wind can
feel.

With the coming-of-age wisdom, it
will only be available to those who
have cherished time as their most
sacred possession.

Buddha was asked, "What have you gained
from meditation?" He replied, "Nothing!"
Then he continued, "However
let me tell you what I have lost:
anger, anxiety, depression,
insecurity and fear of
old age and death."

BUDDHA

Echo In the Wind

A thought that had escaped our
minds resurfaced, bringing us into
self-awareness, the echoes of our
impressions.

A voice whispered to our souls as
time slipped through our hands,
awakening us and aging us beyond
our will, to become the echo of our
forgotten moments.

A spark of passion burns through our
broken hearts as love awakens us,
igniting our smoldering emotions
that echo their light in the darkness
of our souls.

A vision of night ran through our
timeless world as the light of dawn
awakened us to the beauty of half-
forgotten dreams that echo from
the walls of time.

A life lived with purpose has found
eternal meaning in our hearts and has
awakened us to search for ourselves,
here and beyond, in our echo of
silence.

A heart that sings the music of love
becomes the symphony of sound
echoing in the wind, charming the
beloved to come out and dance.

Lost Echo sits amid the voiceless
mountains and feeds her grief.

PERCY BYSSHE SHELLEY

Passing Moments

The infinite moments are but passing
gestures when we smile at them, in
silent reflection, as they slip through
our minds' eyes and escape into the
beyond.

The infinite need for power is our
human folly, as pride sings
louder than words of sincerity.

Infinite love is the heart of creation,
giving us warmth and light to feel
the beauty of our passing moments.

The infinite colors are the eyes of
Nature, as our mind paints it with
many shades of poetic verses on the
canvas of our minds.

The infinite acts of kindness are like
waves of emotions that come to the
shores of our hearts to wash away
the vices of our human nature.

The infinite will of the universe is
embedded in time, moving our minds
to seek the reason for its expanding
curiosity.

We're all born with infinite potential and creativity.
We all have it in us. Each and every
one of us. That's the only truth.

DEEPAK CHOPRA

To Seek Within

It is within time that we see
ourselves in the most splendid ways
reflected within the beauty of life on
the surface of consciousness.

Within life's journey, we walk away
from ourselves to seek and search for
our other half coming our way.

We dream of finding true happiness
between night and day, only to be
awakened by the reality of
perception layered in time.

Within the pages of our conscious
mind, we seek wisdom in our
thoughts, which bind our will to the
world to write the story of our
existence.

In the darkness, we discover the
many shades of light that unveil our
vision, allowing our eyes to see the
true nature of our humanity.

Within the spirit of reflection, we
will find the purpose of our being
descending into the roots of our
beginning.

The struggle within ourselves and
the war to overcome our weaknesses
will ultimately determine the fate of
our humanity.

The greatest battle is the one fought within oneself.

MAHABHARATA

Said Who

I will shield you from the torments
of your conscious mind, said the
spirit to your weary soul.

I will heal you from your moments
of sorrow, said the heart to your
wounded emotions.

I will ask you to forgive those who
harbor wickedness and shower them with
kindness to wash away the darkness
from their eyes.

I will praise the soul that moves us to
lift our burden of reality, said life to
your willful courage.

I will open your eyes to the sublime
beauty of Nature's landscape, said
love in silent wonder to your
mystical gaze.

I will humble my will to your moral
virtues, said wisdom to your
unyielding fate.

I will reach your end when you see
my beginning, said memories to your
forgotten time.

Everything has been said before, but since nobody listens, we have to keep going back and beginning all over again.

ANDRE GIDE

Fully Revealed

Let us love the beauty of life that
takes us deep into time and gives us
the freedom to grow into the
blossoming world.

Let us voice the poetic truth of our
wisdom, which takes us deep into the
mind of our existence, emerging
fully formed.

Let us see the vision in the color of
Nature's light, which will reveal
deep, layered hues within our fully
formed vision.

Let us move along the path of
humanity, seeking the footsteps that
will lead us to spiritual salvation,
fully transformed.

Let us break down the barriers of
human ignorance by seeking
knowledge that will fully reveal our
life's wisdom.

Let us embark on our journey with a
silent mind, voicing the wonder of
our universe entirely to ourselves.

Those things that nature denied to human
sight; she revealed to the
eyes of the soul.

OVID

Walled In

We become trapped in our bodies the
moment we house ourselves inside
the pleasures of our world and lock
ourselves within.

We become trapped in time the
moment we lose the conscious
reality of this world in our perception
of time.

We become trapped in our will when
we sacrifice the power of freedom to
the world, leaving us with no room
to bargain.

We become trapped in our minds
when we lose sight of reality and the
world around us, without conscious
thought.

We become trapped in the blindness
of life the moment we lose sight of
the wisdom that others will come to
take from our world.

We become trapped in the heart of
mischief the moment we destroy our
love for humanity, leaving us no
bridge to cross.

Once you believe things are permanent, you're trapped in a world without doors.

UNKNOWN

Can't Escape

Let the mind hold us within our
consciousness, preventing us from
escaping our awareness of ourselves.

Let the spirit hold us within our souls
by not letting the body escape from
its thirst for living in boundless time.

Let the truth hold us within our
virtues and not escape from our
nature by acting against our human
freedom.

Let the beauty of love hold us within
our emotions, not trying to escape
the lure of its mystical charm.

Let the journey of our mind hold us
within the boundaries of time by not
letting us escape the curiosity of what we
seek in our spirit.

Let the fragrance of life hold us
within our conscious sense by not
letting it escape into the moving
wind.

How shall a man escape from that which is written?
How shall he flee from his destiny?

FERDOWSI

Solitude

I am never alone when you are
closest to me said the shadow to the
light of your being.

I am never alone when you are
closest to me said the body to the
soul of your existence.

I am never alone when you are
closest to me, said Nature to your
loving eyes.

I am never alone when you are
closest to me said the spirit of
wisdom to your conscious mind.

I am never alone when you are
closest to me, said time to the beauty
of your youthful charm.

I am never alone when you are
closest to me, said love to your
beating heart.

I am never alone when you are
dearest to me, said the voice to your
loving words.

Then stirs the feeling infinite, so felt in solitude,
where we are least alone.

LORD BYRON

I Realized

I know your mind delves into
thoughts of evil, but I have given you
the wisdom never to let you go there
without warning.

I know you can reach the peak of
your humanity, for I have given you
the stamina of spirit to get you there
with fortitude.

I know that the passion of love brews
in your soul, for the river of life
flows through your heart and will get
you there with ease.

I know that the mirror of truth
reflects in your eyes, for I have given
you the vision to see you there with
humility in your gaze.

I know the journey through time is
long, but I have told your body to
take its first step to get you there.

I know the dust of your fate is
scattered by the wind, which will
show you the direction to get you
there.

All know that the drop merges into the ocean
but few know that the ocean
merges into the drop.

KABIR

Ashes In Fire

We set fire to the body that houses
our soul; what will we do with the
ashes that blow into the wind?

We set fire to the love that houses
our hearts; what will we do with the
ashes that settle in our emotions?

We set fire to the world that houses
our humanity; what will we do with
the ashes that rain upon our spirit
with regret?

We set fire to the good that houses
our wisdom; what will we do with
the ashes that burn us with hate?

We set fire to the vision that houses
our dreams; what will we do with the
ashes that burn through our
consciousness?

We set fire to the ocean that houses
our thirst; what will we do with the
ashes that hold no water?

We set fire to the mind that houses
our curiosity; what will we do with
the ashes that burn in our
imagination?

The mind is not a vessel to be filled, but a fire to be kindled.

PLUTARCH

Silent Whisper

We are born with eyes to see, as the
light gives us the vision to move
toward life's journey through our
conscious mind.

The will of humanity molds us, but
the love of spirit gives us the grace to
create the life we crave in our hearts.

The whisper of Nature's calling
awakens us, but it is in silent
reflection that dreams become a
reality for our eyes to see.

We are moved by the will of time,
but our conscious freedom
determines our worldly purpose in
the flux of our existence.

The wisdom of our needs is self-
fulfilling, as the wants of this world
lure us with life's eternal pleasures.

We are the seekers of human
understanding who seeks but never
find the seeking nature of our
existence.

Silence is the element in which great things fashion themselves together.

THOMAS CARLYLE

Eyes That See

The vision of reality settles in our
consciousness as our mind awakens
us to mystical wonder.

The vision of curiosity awakens our
eyes as thoughts take flight under the
wings of our imagination.

The vision of truth awakens our
moral voice when the sound of
wisdom reaches the conscious world.

The vision of light awakens us from
our darkness, the moment we
embrace the colors of Nature's
beauty with our infinite shades of
emotions.

The vision of love awakens us
toward life's purpose as we take our
first step toward self-fulfillment.

The vision of our inner eye awakens
us to our external reality as the veil
of consciousness lifts us from our
world.

Your vision will become clear only when you can look into your own heart. Who looks outside, dreams; who looks inside, awakes.

CARL JUNG

Rays of Light

In the dawn of light, the spirit
awakens to the majestic voice of
Nature's calling with silent wonder.

In the warm rays of the rising sun,
the world will awaken to the
melodious birdsong with a
welcoming heart.

In the silence of our humble mind,
the human spirit will remain
motionless in the streams of moving
time flowing through its
consciousness.

In the veil of darkness, the night will
blanket the world in its mystical
dreams under the shades of the
glowing moonlight.

In the twilight of mystical silence,
time will wash the beauty of our
worldly existence with the dust of
starlight.

The depth of imagination will reflect
the blue sea of the open sky in our
eyes, drowning us in its deep
reflection.

Concentrate all your thoughts upon the work at hand. The sun's rays do not burn until brought to a focus.

ALEXANDER GRAHAM BELL

Wisdom Given

I have chosen you among the living
and sent you time to grow into your
rooted spirit.

I have given you the vision to look
beyond yourself, said wisdom to
your awakened mind.

I have given you the will to walk
beyond your life's journey, said the
soul to your moving feet.

I have whispered the truth of human
morality, said consciousness to your
enlightened Self.

I have given you the virtue to seek
the mystical truth in reality, said
experience to the realm of your
worldly perception.

I have given you the light of mystery
to your soul, said the mirror to your
reflecting eyes.

I have given you the gift of life, said
creation to the blossoming seeds of
your beginning in time.

A gift is pure when it is given from the heart
to the right person at the right time and
at the right place, and when we
expect nothing in return.

BHAGAVAD GITA

Chosen

Our spirit will give us the voice of
our existence, but we choose not to
listen to it when we are determined
in our ways.

Our spirit will race through the eye
of our existence, but our mind's eye
searches without realizing it has
already left through our doors.

Our spirit will return to us with
revelation, but we deny the true
beauty of its nature to our loving
souls.

Our spirit will guide our every step,
but we stumble, causing us to run in
circles until we fall to the ground
exhausted.

Our spirit will reflect the glow of our
existence, but we quickly drown that
light in the world's darkness, which
veils our eyes.

Our spirit will tell the story of life,
but we forget to write the
impressions that are etched by the
whim of time.

Our spirit will choose the one created
for us, but we decide to run into the
arms of the one who does not love
us.

You did not choose me, but I chose you.

JOHN 15:16

Vision of Light

Into the way of our open path in life,
we shall find all we want when we
consciously walk through time
seeking ourselves.

Into the way of our minds, our
thoughts will guide us into action the
moment they come into our
conscious awareness.

Into the beauty of love, our hearts
shall seek the one walking toward us
with light in their eyes.

Into the vision, we search for light;
our eyes will gaze into the horizon,
seeking the reflection that reveals
our hidden fate.

Into the deep stillness of the night,
our dreams will become a reality the
moment conscious time whispers our
name.

Into the farthest reaches of our
imagination, our perception of
wonder will return to us, mesmerized
by our mind's reflection.

The only thing worse than being blind is having sight but no vision.

HELEN KELLER

Held Close

I will keep you close to my heart,
voice the mind to your spirit when
the world is no longer real.

I will keep you within my sight, the
soul whispered to your human
nature, when you open your eyes to
the world you have left behind.

I will continue to love you with total
devotion, as Nature voices to you
the beauty of your humble spirit.

I will keep whispering the words you
long to hear, voicing wisdom to the
awakening of your conscious mind.

I will keep shedding light into your
soul, voiced the body to the shadow
of your form.

I will keep paving the path toward
your fate, guided by the will of your
moving spirit.

I will continue to bring joy into your
laughter, voicing the life you have
created within yourself.

Keep your face always toward the sunshine
and shadows will fall behind you.

WALT WHITMAN

Spirit To Be

The will to be is who we want to be,
molded by how we think and wish to
be.

The will to be is the moment we take
our first step into the world that we
hope it to be.

The will to be shall be the moment
we voice our moral courage into a
world that we want it to be.

The will to be shall be the moment
we are loved by the spirit that wills
us to be.

The will to be shall be the moment
we open our eyes to the beauty of
this world that loves us to be.

The will to be is the moment we
reflect in the mirror of reality, seeing
ourselves as we hope to be.

The will to be is the fate of our
human nature that comes into us to
let us be.

There is a candle in your heart, ready to be kindled. There is a void in your soul, ready to be filled. You feel it, don't you?

RUMI

Reborn

The resurrection of your spirit occurs
when the metamorphosis of your
morality is reborn into your
existence, illuminated by the light of
your heart.

The resurrection of your conscious
mind awakens you the moment you
fall in love with the beauty of your
conscious existence.

The resurrection of being human is
to live within the space of time by
holding sacred the purpose of your
worldly journey.

The resurrection of your faith brings
harmony to your spirit by washing
your face with the purity of holy water.

The resurrection of truth comes the
moment you seek wisdom by
humbling yourself to the virtue of
being humane.

The resurrection of humanity is the
birth of morality rooted in our spirit's
rising to the surface of our
consciousness.

Our greatest ability as humans is not to change the world, but to change ourselves.

MAHATMA GANDHI

Chapter 6: Darkness, Light, Good, and Evil

Let there be wisdom in good that will show us the light to overcome the darkness of our evil nature. The evils of the world are what we must mirror to humanity and awaken their collective consciousness to uphold human virtue. The many shades of reality become etched in our minds, and the only light we see is the one that opens our consciousness. The vision of morality is to see through the veil of darkness and live a life of moral courage by defending the sanctity of good against evil.

Darkness will cast no light when our eyes remain closed as we walk into the world without conscious reflection. True wisdom lies in taming our human emotions and conquering the Self, lost in the uncertainty of time. Blessed is the spirit that fights the enemy within and lights the candle to help us see the darkness of our human ways. The good of our spirit will always conquer evil when we destroy it with kindness and love.

The beauty of light will shine in our conscious eyes, revealing to us our hidden nature, which harbors evil. The darkness that blinds our spirit, the light of wisdom, will bring us to see. The many shades of our moral character will be reflected in our moments of conscious reflection.

The light will glaze our surface of reality; the wisdom of life will reveal the perception of what our mind seeks to understand. The virtues of knowing and not knowing will humble the soul and give the spirit the light to seek simplicity. "Many Shades of Wisdom" is the moral compass that guides us toward living in righteous ways and gives evil no room to enter our souls.

Hate can only burn the one who hates, like a fire that consumes your spirit when it touches your heart.

SHAKOOR

One Moment

Light searches for its lost love for a
thousand years, only to sacrifice its
soul to the darkness of eternity.

For a thousand years, the beauty of
Nature has remained hidden from the
naked eye of creation, only to be
plucked away by the hands of time.

For a thousand years, the mind
evolved into the lucidity of human
reasoning, only to regress into the
tribal nature of its primitive past.

For a thousand years, the dust of
history settles at the feet of
civilization, only to be blown away
by the storms of human emotions.

For a thousand years, love has grown
into the heart of creation, only to
walk away with the fragrance of
life.

For a thousand years, humanity has
been at war with itself, only to find
peace once it has destroyed
everything it has built.

The universe moves toward eternity
for a thousand years, only to implode
upon time and space.

For a thousand years, life has grown
into the soul of humanity, only to be
destroyed by the burning passions of
our hearts.

The reputation of a thousand years may be determined by the conduct of one hour.

CONFUCIUS

Not Afraid

There is no fear of darkness when
the light of wisdom glows in our
hearts to reveal our path toward life.

There is no fear of uncertainty when
faith is the most certain thing known
to our souls to help us walk out into
the world.

There is no fear of sorrow when we
strive for a better world tomorrow by
reflecting on what we will do today.

There is no fear of death when the
life that we live is sacrificed for the
greater good, for the betterment of
others.

There is no fear in telling the truth
when we break our will to uphold
our moral virtue by standing up to
the hypocrisy of our human ways.

There is no fear in taking our first
step into the world when it helps us
grow with time and fulfill the
purpose of our mortal existence.

There is no fear of entering the cave
of darkness when you dispel it with
the light that emanates from your
heart.

The cave you fear to enter may hold
the light you seek.

RUMI

Ask Me Not

Forgive me not if I can't forgive
those who have done me wrong.

Love me not if I can't love those who
love me least.

Hear me not if I can break the silence
of those who hide under their hateful
motives.

See me not if I can't open the eyes of
those who live in blindness.

Touch me not if I can't extinguish the
evil in souls that burn with hate.

Call me not if I can't offer my hand
of friendship to my enemies who
lurk all around.

Praise me not if I can't give you my
humble wisdom with my virtuous
heart.

Embrace me not if I can't give up the
wealth of my spirit to those who are
poor in their moral ways.

Judge me not if I can't sacrifice
myself for the greater good of
humanity.

Go not to the temple to put flowers upon the feet of God; first fill your own house with the fragrance of love. Go not to the temple to light candles before the altar of God; first remove the darkness of sin from your heart. Go not to the temple to bow down your head in prayer; first learn to bow in humility before your fellow men. Go not to the temple to pray on bent knees first; bend down to lift someone who is downtrodden. Go not to the temple to ask for forgiveness for your sins; first, forgive from your heart those who have sinned against you.

RABINDRANATH TAGORE

Root of Evil

Evil will burn away the goodness of
our hearts, and blindness will prevail
in the darkness of our worldly ways.

Evil will remain naked to our
conscious eye, and there will be no
place for it to hide.

Evil will be conquered by the truth
the moment it is revealed and seen
by the light of human dignity.

Evil can never shatter our will, for
the spirit of freedom will never be
oppressed by the power of tyranny.

Will we pull out the roots of evil and
never let them take hold in our
souls?

The wrath of evil will destroy
humanity, becoming a disease that
plagues its conscience.

The thought of good is to do no evil;
only then will love and compassion
seep into your soul.

You do not do evil to those who do evil to you, but you deal with them, with forgiveness and kindness.

PROPHET MUHAMMAD (PBUH)

Moral Act

The birth of our spirit is made pure
gold and becomes most precious in
the hands of creation.

Doing good deeds will bring you
peace and fulfillment on your long
journey through time.

The sins of humanity are washed
away by the love we give to those
who have harmed us.

Love one another, and the greater
love will keep our faith strong and
carry us through hard times.

The great wisdom you reflect on the
world is the character of your
conduct toward others.

Wash your hate in the purity of love,
and the sweetness will linger on your
lips for all eternity.

The great folly in life is when you
put your hand in the fire and think it
will not burn.

The moral act will build civilization,
raise them above their conscious
horizon, and help them see the
beauty in the unity of spirit.

Your own soul is nourished when you are kind; it is destroyed when you are cruel.

KING SOLOMON

A Lifetime

For a thousand years, light seeks
purpose in the darkness of reality,
but finds the shadow still lurks in
humanity's blind ways.

For a thousand years, the mystery of
Nature remains hidden from our
consciousness, only to be revealed to
the eye that seeks it with its mystical
mind.

For a thousand years, the soul
evolved into the spirit of being
human, only to crumble under the
lures of worldly pleasures.

For a thousand years, the dust of
time settles at the feet of civilization,
only to be blown away by the storms
of human passion.

For a thousand years, the will of
humanity has journeyed through the
world in search of itself, only to find
that it is lost in the pleasures of
worldly comforts.

For a thousand years, the wisdom of
beauty lay hidden under the veil of
love, only to be embraced once we opened
our hearts to let it in.

It is better to have dreamed a thousand dreams that never were than never to have dreamed at all.

ALEXANDER PUSHKIN

Will To Act

We work toward the good of
humanity the moment we take
responsibility for our mortal
existence.

We work toward the perfection of
our moral Self the moment we
become conscious of our humble
ways.

We work toward creating beauty
when we sow the seeds of truth into
our souls.

We work toward fulfilling our life's
purpose when we take on the task of
our worldly obligations.

We work toward the grace of
humility the moment we give
ourselves to the furtherance of
others.

We worked to improve our minds by
pursuing knowledge that reveals the
wisdom inherent in our human
nature.

We work to perfect our character by
reflecting on the imperfections we
see in ourselves.

Take every effort to guard your tongue as
it is the strongest cause for your
destruction in this
life and the next.

AL-GHAZALI

Act of Kindness

Through the act of goodness in our
hearts, we become the beacon of
hope for humanity that has gone
astray.

We can heal the ailing body through
goodness and compassion by curing
the sickly mind infected with hate.

Through acts of kindness and intent,
we strive to change the moral
atmosphere of our spiritual world by
remaining calm in our moments of
turmoil.

We learn to love ourselves and
others most lovingly through acts of
kindness emanating from our hearts.

Through the act of goodness from
our souls, we spread the light of
wisdom into the darkness of this
world.

We discover the true nature of
human empathy in the act of
goodness that serves humanity.

An enemy to whom you show kindness
becomes your friend, excepting lust,
the indulgence of which
increases its enmity.

SAADI

Light In Shadow

From darkness into light, we come to
see the reality of our existence only
when we open our eyes to see
ourselves.

The path towards our destiny will be
revealed from darkness into light, the
moment we take our first step out
into the world.

The colors of Nature's beauty will
spill into our spirit from darkness
into light when we awaken from our
dream-like state.

From darkness into light, the shadow
will become one with our form when
we lift the veil from our
consciousness.

We will walk out into the world from
darkness into light, becoming the
vision of reflected time that our eyes
long to see.

The truth will be revealed from
darkness into light when wisdom
seals the cracks in the crumbling
certainty of our world.

Wisdom comes when we walk from
darkness into light by lighting the
candle before our eyes to seek
reality, not its shadow.

Give light, and the darkness will disappear of itself.

DESIDERIUS ERASMUS

Lift The Veil

We have unveiled the face of
humanity, and what we see is the
fading lines of our civilization.

We have unveiled the darkness from
our eyes; we only see the tears of our
silent destruction.

We have unveiled love, which is the
scent of this world, but the fragrance
of life has dissipated into the moving
nature of time.

We have unveiled the unwritten
poetry that is etched in our minds,
but the words of wisdom remain
scattered by the verses of life.

We have unveiled the power of our
evil ways, but the compassionate
soul will slay it with the sword of
kindness.

We have unveiled the hidden
purpose of our existence, but the
stoic nature of our human ways will
not bring it to light.

The unveiling of the truth unveils us
from darkness, but the Self behind
the veil can never be hidden.

For there is nothing hidden that will not become
evident, nor anything secret that will
not be known and come
out into the open.

LUKE 8:17

Spirit of Healing

To be a good physician, you must
first give your patients the
confidence to believe in your healing
spirit and to do no harm.

To be a good physician, you must
offer unconditional love,
compassion and empathy through
your healing art.

To be a good physician, you must
listen to your patients and form a
collaborative partnership to help
each other navigate life's most
challenging moments.

To be a good physician, you must
practice holistic medicine with
wisdom to heal the mind, body, and
soul.

To be a good physician, you must
give your patients the spirit of love
and teach them your healing art.

To be a good physician, you must
remind yourself that you are treating
a human being, not a diagnosis.

The spirit of healing is the art of
medicine; no method can equal its
success.

Make a habit of two things: to help or
at least to do no harm.

HIPPOCRATES

Humbled Grace

We hold compassion in our hearts,
for it helps us live in humble grace,
which takes away the pride in our
ritualistic ways.

We empathize with those who have
wronged us, and forgiveness
strengthens us and liberates our spirit
from the flaws in our nature.

It is the compassion of loving others
by giving them our sacred hearts that
keeps love precious.

The empathy of life's experiences
takes away the uncertainty of time,
making us reflect on the silent
moments of the world we want to
preserve.

The grace of humility makes us
human, giving us the means to look
beyond our narrow horizons when
seeking simplicity in our world.

In empathy, we extend our hand to
humanity to carry them away from
the lure of their wayward ways.

A lamp can only light another lamp when it continues to burn in its own flame.

RABINDRANATH TAGORE

Casting Shadow

Under the shadow of our form rests
the light of mystery that carves our
spirit from the soul of creation.

Under the shadow of our reflection
lies the hidden veil of truth that
comes through the cracks in our
conscious mind.

Under the shadow of our many
shades lies the colors of Nature,
which reveal the beauty of life that
bleeds into our heart's emotions.

Under the shadow of time, life
awakens from its deep slumber and
moves toward a meaningful
existence.

Under the shadow of love, wasted
emotions overflow into our drowning
hearts and will never come to the
surface of our being.

Under the shadow of comfort, the
gentle breeze envelops our spirit,
offering us solace from the world's
unforgiving gaze.

Don't depend too much on anyone in this world because even your own shadow leaves you when you are in darkness.

IBN TAYMIYYAH

Will You See?

Behold, the vision of reality has
been revealed to your eyes; all you
have to do is open your mind and let
it come in.

Behold, the truth of your wisdom is
revealed to your conscious will the
moment you take it in with your
whole being.

Behold, your life is a passing
moment, but if you live it with
righteousness, it will become all-
encompassing when it returns.

Behold, if you fight for the good of
this world, you will have the power
to stand up against the might of
evil.

Behold, if you love passionately, you
will show your soul's purity with
compassion from your heart.

Behold, the spirit of your existence is
the vision of freedom, the force of
your will that sets you free from the
fate of your worldly journey.

Behold, I stand at the door and knock. If anyone hears my voice and opens the door, I will come in to him and eat with him, and he with me.

JESUS CHRIST

What I Became

I will look into the mirror of self-
reflection and ask myself: Who am I,
and what have I become?

I will wait for wisdom to meet my
mind and ask myself: What do I
want to know, and what do I think
that knowledge can reveal?

I will sow the seed of love into her
soul and ask myself: How can love
grow roots in a barren soul that holds
no compassion?

I will dream of a world that holds
sacred the gift of life and ask myself:
What is the purpose of time when
life is wasted on the wastelands of
our dreams?

I will walk the journey that
surrenders my will to freedom and
ask myself: How far will I go to find
myself, and what will I do when we
finally meet?

I will see the vision of light that
awakens my consciousness and ask
myself: What did reality reveal
before and after the coming of
darkness?

Whoever acquires knowledge but does not practice it is as one who ploughs but does not sow.

SAADI

Art of Virtue

In the goodness of our hearts, we
gather the masses to bring them into
the unity of one spirit and one soul.

In the grandness of our deeds, we are
bound to our gracious acts to serve
and invoke the sentiments of our
humanity.

In the goodness of our virtues, we
defend the moral truth of our wisdom
and serve the sacred faith of our
inner convictions.

In the grandness of our spirit, we
gaze at the world in the face of
darkness and bring light into the
blindness of our human ways.

In the goodness of our minds, we
seek the creativity of our imagination
to change our perception of reality.

In the grandeur of our actions, we
bring momentum to civilization,
which has been shackled by
worldly greed.

A tree is known by its fruit, a man by his deeds. A good deed is never lost; he who sows courtesy reaps friendship, and he who plants kindness gathers love.

UNKNOWN

With Whom?

Whom shall we call when the path to
our destiny has been erased by time?

Whom shall we see when we look in
the mirror of self-reflection and see
no wisdom in our vision?

Whom shall we fear when the
darkness of our ways has been
revealed to the eyes of the world?

Whom shall we trust when we open
our doors to humanity that no longer
holds empathy in their hearts?

Whom shall we love when the heart
no longer beats in harmony with our
emotions?

Whom shall we allow to enter a
world where the shadow of evil lurks
in the background of our human
nature?

Whom shall we follow when we
declare war within ourselves and
can't make peace with the civility of
our humble Self?

Accept the things to which fate binds you, and love the people with whom fate brings you together, but do so with all your heart.

MARCUS AURELIUS

I Shall Keep

Keep loving with your whole spirit;
one day, love will walk into your
heart with humble grace.

Keep striving toward the path you
seek; one day, you shall reach your
destination with your willful steps.

Keep dreaming of the life you want
to live; one day, the fruit of your
hard work will bring it to reality.

Keep your eyes open to the wisdom
of Nature; one day, the vision of
beauty will pour into your empty
soul.

Keep fighting for the good of human
virtues; one day, the grace of
humanity will become the soul of
your moral being.

Keep hope burning in the darkness of
your mind; one day, the light of faith
will set you free.

Keep pointing the finger in the
direction your fate will take; one day,
the journey of a lifetime will fulfill
your dreams.

Keep your eyes on the stars, and
your feet on the ground.

THEODORE ROOSEVELT

Afraid Not

Fear not, for I will guard your
wisdom and faith in your wandering
spirit with the courage of my mind.

Fear not, for I will guard your
beauty, said love to your faithful
heart.

Fear not, for I will guard your body,
said time to your aging soul.

Fear not, for I will guard your
happiness by spreading joy into your
suffering Self.

Fear not, for I will guard your vision,
said light to the darkness encircled in
your eyes.

Fear not, for I will guard your
dreams, said the night to your mind's
drifting consciousness.

Fear not, for I will guard your light,
said the candle to your growing
shadow of uncertainty.

We can easily forgive a child who is afraid
of the dark; the real tragedy of life
is when men are afraid
of the light.

PLATO

Lurking Soul

Fear me not, for I shall lurk in your
consciousness where evil fears you
most when you are morally strong.

See me not, for I shall lurk in your
darkness where the light sees you
most when your eyes are not blind to
the world.

Forget me not, for I shall lurk in your
thoughts where the mind feels you
most when you are conscious of
yourself.

Leave me not, for I shall lurk in your
spirit where the soul needs you most
when you are lost in your ways.

Waste me not, for I shall lurk in your
body where the vigor of life protects
you most when the ills of this world
infect your spirit.

Hear me not, for I shall lurk in your
silence where the voice listens to you
most when you have become deaf to
the sound of your wisdom.

Maybe you have to know the darkness before you can appreciate the light.

MADELEINE L'ENGLE

In Harmony

Keep peace close to your heart and
let no one enter it who will do you
wrong.

Keep peace in your conscious
thoughts, and let no words sway you
from your spoken truth.

Keep peace between your body and
soul; let the two become one with
your spiritual world.

Keep peace with the harmony of
your spirit, and let the inner calm
wash away the storms of your human
emotions.

Keep peace with your mortal enemy,
and your love for humanity will
sway them with kindness.

Keep peace with your human nature
and make it fall in love with your
soul that will harmonize your
conscious being.

Keep peace with the world that has
gone astray, and the grace of your
wisdom will find them their
righteous path in life.

Happiness is when what you think, what you say, and what you do is in harmony.

MAHATMA GANDHI

Power of Will

The power of our words is a greater
force that will cut through the fog of
evil surrounding our worldly ways.

The strength of our character is the
beacon of light that will guide the
souls to the one who has awakened
us from the darkness of our ways.

The power of love will thaw our
slumbering emotions and warm our
hearts with the beauty of the all-
encompassing grace.

The strength of wisdom will give us
the courage to navigate life's storms
and reach the calm of our inner
world.

The power of privilege corrupts the
mind when it oppresses the freedom
of those who gave it to us to use
wisely.

The strength of humanity lies in our
collective consciousness, which
holds sacred the sanctity of life under
the guiding spirit of morality.

What emerges from the heart has an impact,
even if it lacks force, though it lacks the
strength to soar, it has the
power to influence.

MIRZA GHALIB

Chapter 7: Wealth, Health, Poverty, Power, and Fame

All the world's great fortunes can't measure up against one ounce of good health. Life is a journey through time, the poverty of our spirit enriched by the beauty of our simple ways. The power of our will guides us in the world, providing the momentum to move and seek our purpose in what we aspire to be. The more we have, the less we keep when the time comes to take it all away.

The hoarding of wealth is a manifestation of human greed, and the flaunting of it makes you a target in the envious eyes of the world. We are all fated to one end, and when it comes, we are all humbled in silence and liberated from our needs. We are born and left empty; all we gain will become other people's treasures. The simpler you make your life, the richer your existence will be, and the more time you invest in yourself.

No power can bargain with time; everything comes and goes. No fame in our fortune will keep the flame burning forever. The higher you climb, the steeper you fall when you falter. You will be measured by what you give and not by what you have.

The wealth of your spirit will become the fortune of your wisdom, enriching your life. The poverty of your needs will become the many characteristics of your human nature that will enhance your soul and give you more time to live. "Many Shades of Wisdom" becomes your life's fortune that no one can take from you.

The fortunes you seek are within yourself, but why do you look for them in all the wrong places?

SHAKOOR

Wealth of Being

A wounded pride bears the scars of
vanity, but humility will bring back
your humanity by its wisdom of
healing your spirit.

A joyful life can bear the burden of
time and free the soul from the
heaviness of needs by uplifting the
spirit from the lure of the world's
pleasures.

A soulful person can find treasures in
the simplest things by letting go of
what they do not need.

A curious mind can see beyond the
reality of this world by letting its
imagination lift the veil from the
consciousness of life.

A welcoming spirit can see the
mystical beauty in life by opening
the door to the one it loves the most.

A loving soul can change the world
by bringing the candle of light to
wash away the darkness.

A joyful laughter can ease the
world's sorrow and give life the rays
of hope that will illuminate the soul
of humanity.

He is the richest who is content with the least, for content is the wealth of nature.

SOCRATES

Never-ending

The human spirit, consumed by
worldly pleasures, becomes a slave
to insatiable desires, imprisoning its
soul in the trappings of the world.

The complexity of life traps the soul
and leaves the spirit empty, like a
dormant seed with no chance of
awakening.

We long for love, but our selfish
desires bleed into the heart, leaving it
no longer capable of love.

In our greed, we sell our human
virtues for the wealth of this world,
which robs us of time we can never
get back.

Our appetite for wealth and greed is
more profound than any ocean, and
the need for more will forever keep
us thirsty.

Why do we seek power that burdens
our souls and will take us to our end
with conscious speed?

The never-ending nature of our
human pleasures are the fire that will
never stop burning in our smoldering
greed.

The world is big enough to satisfy everyone's needs, but it will always be too small to satisfy everyone's greed

MAHATMA GANDHI

There, I Am

Therefore, I tell you that you have
the power to change yourself, and
through yourself, you can change the
world.

Therefore, I tell you that you can
stand up for the moral truth only
when you break your silence and
speak your truth with your moral
voice.

Therefore, I tell you that you can
walk a thousand-mile journey with
one step the moment you dare to
move beyond yourself.

Therefore, I tell you that you have
the vision to inspire the world when
you take your pen and write the
poetry of your imagination.

Therefore, I tell you that you can
only love someone when you remove
yourself from the pride and envy of
wanting to be loved.

Therefore, I tell you that the beauty
of love is sacred to the heart when
you give without the desire to want it
back.

See, I have set before you this day life and good,
death and evil . . . I have set before you life
and death, blessing and curse;
therefore, choose life.

MOSES

Power To Be

In the power of your will, you can
live your life to the fullest by your
means when you let go of what you
don't need.

In the power of your will, you can
move through the world with
lightness in mind and a steady pace
toward your conscious journey.

In the power of your will, your fate
can be written by the virtuous actions
of your deeds in the world.

In the power of your will, you can
give your spirit the freedom to touch
all aspects of human experience.

In the power of your will, you can let
go of your passion for wealth and
move toward a life of simplicity.

In the power of your will, you can
spend time searching for yourself to
find what is searching for you.

In the power of your will, you can
climb the highest mountain, but
remain humble enough to return
back to your base.

We have more ability than willpower, and it is often an excuse to ourselves that we imagine that things are impossible.

FRANCOIS DE LA ROCHEFOUCAULD

The Fight Within

The war within our conscious soul is
the mortal conflict we must
overcome to conquer ourselves from
ourselves.

Human nature will destroy
everything it touches when it pursues
the power, fame, and fortune of this
world till the end of time.

Human nature is most destructive
when it does not realize the power of
its wicked mind until its destructive
will entirely consume it.

The path to annihilation is only
realized when we devour and burn
all we love in a house that we have
built for ourselves.

The good of humanity is the light in
our world that will reveal all the
darkness of power in our evil ways.

Where there is human dignity, there
shall be peace, but where there is
tyranny of war, there shall remain
the shadow of suffering.

Within and outside of us is the path
to moral goodness that we must
battle through to find the truth when
seeking the Self.

If you know neither the enemy nor yourself, you will succumb in every battle

SUN TZU

Be Content

We can never find peace when we
hold the venom of hate and envy of
others in our hearts.

We can never find peace when we
chase power with our whole being
and become powerless in its ever-
tightening grip upon our moral
judgments.

We can never find peace if we run
around the world looking for
something that does not exist.

We can never find peace if we hoard
wealth and become consumed by our
ever-growing need for fulfillment.

We can only find peace when we
accept what we have and let go of
what serves no purpose.

We can only find peace when we are
content with something less than
something more.

We can only find peace when we
seek humility and walk away from
our pride, leaving our footsteps behind.

Be content with what you have; rejoice in the way things are. When you realize there is nothing lacking, the whole world belongs to you.

LAO TZU

Be On Guard

Guard against the thieves of this
world, for they will rob your wealth
and soul under the cover of darkness.

Guard against the vanity of your
mind, for it will make you a fool in
the pride of your worldly actions.

Guard against the evils of this world,
for they will take away your
humanity with no conscious
afterthought in doing you harm.

Guard against the lies of this world,
for they will keep you blind and
ignorant in the vision of truth.

Guard against the power of your
perception, for it will lead you astray
into the reality of illusions that will
betray your conscious mind.

Guard against the passions in your
heart, for they will consume you in
the fire of emotions you cannot put
out.

Above all else, guard your heart, for everything you do flows from it.

PROVERBS 4:23

Self-power

The power of our will moves us
beyond the boundaries of our reach
as long as we believe in the capacity
of our being.

The power of our mind will
encompass our universe as long as
we can use our imagination to reach
the very edge of our consciousness.

The power of our spirit will elevate
us beyond our wisdom as long as we
have the freedom to defend the truth
that lives within our hearts.

The power to conquer yourself is the
measure of true strength in your
character; all other things will make
you powerless.

The power of our words shall
awaken the human spirit as long as
we give it the wisdom to remain
steadfast in our righteous ways.

The power of good over evil is like
light over darkness as long as it gives
us the courage to defend the sanctity
of our living truth.

The power of compassion is the
soul of humanity as long as we give
it the empathy of our loving hearts.

Mastering others is a strength, mastering
yourself is true power.

TAO TE CHING

Remain Strong

Stand firm in your beliefs, for it is
the only thing that will keep you on
solid ground.

Stand firm against the tyranny of
evil, for it is the only thing that can
preserve the immortal soul.

Stand firm against the power of
greed, for it is the only thing that will
strengthen your character.

Stand firm against inequality, for it is
the only dividing element that will
fragment your human spirit.

Stand firm against the cruelty of
human nature, for it is the only thing
that will prolong your suffering and
hasten your demise.

Stand firm against yourself, for it is
the only way to change what you
wish not to become.

Stand firm against the uncertainty of
doubt, for it is the only perception
that will not move you forward.

Be sure you put your feet in the right place, then stand firm.

ABRAHAM LINCOLN

Of Being Human

The spirit of humanity will engulf us
in worldly pleasures when it
surrenders willfully to the carnal
nature of our human emotions.

The spirit of humanity will open its
eyes to the light of wisdom, which
will lay the path toward the unity of
our human vision.

The spirit of humanity will remain in
chaos when it runs in all directions,
seeking fulfillment in power that it
can't sustain.

The spirit of humanity is lost to the
world that does not value the beauty
of love when it sells itself to the
buyers of this world.

The spirit of humanity will decay
when it takes away the freedom of
others and holds them prisoners
against their will.

The spirit of humanity will never rise
against the power of evil when it
remains silent under the wrath of its
devastating effects on humankind.

My humanity is bound up in yours, for we can only be human together.

DESMOND TUTU

Serenity In Peace

You can never find peace when you
grow the poison of hate for others in
your heart with unconscious fury.

You can never find peace when you
chase power with your being that
casts a mighty shadow upon your
moral judgments.

You can never find peace if you run
around the world seeking pleasures
that can never fulfill your existence.

You can never find peace if you seek
treasures, which take you deeper into
your unmarked grave the moment
they are yours.

You can only find peace when you
cherish what you have and give
others what you don't need within
your lifetime.

You can only find peace when you
humble yourself before the ground
that holds you up to the world.

You will find peace when you make
peace with yourself; that is the only
piece that will bring you peace.

Here, the ways of men divide. If you wish to strive for peace of soul and happiness, then believe; if you wish to be a disciple of truth, then inquire.

FRIEDRICH NIETZSCHE

Being Fulfilled

The contentment of will can be
achieved once you let go of the
needs of this world that keep
knocking at your door.

The contentment of purpose will
give you a moment of solace when
you pursue the beauty of life that
will come to embrace your spirit.

The contentment in who you are will
lead to wisdom the moment you
consciously accept the humble fate
of your mortal existence.

The contentment in fame, wealth,
and fortune can never be attained
until you walk away from them with
empty hands.

The contentment of your mind will
ease your thoughts when your
intelligence is in harmony with your
conscious world.

The contentment of your thirst for
pleasure will never satisfy you until
you savor what you have as your
most cherished virtue.

Do not spoil what you have by desiring what you have not; remember that what you now have was once among the things you only hoped for.

EPICURUS

By SHAKOOR

Index

www.ingramcontent.com/pod-product-compliance
Lightning Source LLC
LaVergne TN
LVHW050627100826
845148LV00011B/1757

* 9 7 9 8 3 8 5 2 7 2 8 5 3 *